The
HEALING
LANDSCAPE

The
HEALING
LANDSCAPE

Therapeutic Outdoor Environments

Martha M. Tyson

McGraw-Hill

New York San Francisco Washington, D.C. Auckland Bogotá Caracas Lisbon London Madrid
Mexico City Milan Montreal New Delhi San Juan Singapore Sydney Tokyo Toronto

Library of Congress Cataloging-in-Publication Data

Tyson, Martha M.
      The healing landscape : therapeutic outdoor environments / Martha
M. Tyson.
            p.   cm.
      Includes bibliographical references (p.   ) and index.
      ISBN 0-07-065768-8
      1. Gardening—Therapeutic use. I. Title.
RM735.7.G37T97   1998
615.8'515—dc21

97-39993
CIP

McGraw-Hill

A Division of The **McGraw·Hill** Companies

1 2 3 4 5 6 7 8 9 0 KGP/KGP 9 0 3 2 1 0 9 8

ISBN: 0-07-065768-8

*The sponsoring editor for this book was Wendy Lochner, the editing supervisor
was Ruth Mannino, and the production supervisor was Sherri Souffrance. It was
designed and set in Avenir by Ron Lane and Vincent Piazza of McGraw-Hill's
desktop publishing department, New York, N.Y.*

Printed and bound by Quebecor/Kingsport.

This book is printed on acid-free paper.

Daniel Alpert

This book is dedicated to Prof. Natalie Alpert (1920–1997),

The University of Illinois at Urbana-Champaign

"You have found the good fortune to find real teachers, authentic friends, who have taught you everything you wanted to know without holding back. You have had no need to steal their knowledge, because they led you along the easiest path, even though it had cost them a lot of hard work and suffering to discover it. Now it is your turn to do the same, with one person, and another—with everyone." —J. Escrivá, 1988

CONTENTS

Lilacs in bloom (Mike Jones).

PREFACE

Vince Healy, a colleague from San Francisco is a pioneer in the design of healing gardens. Vince has kindly consented to my relating some of his anecdotes about the healing power of flowers and their fragrances.

In one such anecdote, Vince described a visit to his grandmother at a nursing home. Vince's grandmother was in her nineties. For quite some time she had not recognized Vince and was not really fully aware of what was going on around her. Since it was Easter time, Vince decided to pay her a visit. During his drive there, Vince came upon a roadside stand that advertised lilacs for sale. In southern California, lilacs do not grow well. This stand, however, had great quantities of them, and they were cheap. So Vince bought an enormous number of the lilacs and put them in the back of his van. Back on the road again, Vince immediately slammed into a traffic jam that lasted about four hours.

By the time Vince arrived at the nursing home, the lilacs were looking very sad. When Vince walked into his grandmother's room, she looked at him as always, blankly, and then she looked at the flowers. "They're wilted! Throw them away!" After all his effort Vince was not about to throw them away, so he moved the lilacs closer, right under her nose. She drew in the fragrance with a deep breath and a sigh and said, "Lilacs...." Then she looked up at Vince and said, "*Vinnie*, how *are* you?" The fragrance literally had brought her back to reality.

Apparently, the sense of smell is directly connected to the limbic system, accounting for the remarkable ability of specific smells to recall old memories.

In terms of patients in hospice settings, Vince explained that some patients suffer from *anosmias*, the inability to smell, while others are so sensitized that almost any fragrance will induce vomiting. However, he added that most patients can enjoy the garden's fragrances. For individuals whose sense of smell remains impaired, any fragrance that is familiar will arouse memories, some good and some bad, depending on the associations. Unfortunately, some illnesses and some treatments, especially chemotherapy, render any smell at all nauseating. Thus, a very delicate balance must be maintained as to how and where you place fragrances.

Nancy Gerlach is working on a project at Queens Village, a Catholic convalescent hospital for the elderly. Oliver Sacks, the neurologist, took Nancy and Vince to the Queen of Peace Hospital. As he was escorting them around, there was a twinkle in his eye; it was apparent that he would *really* like to see something positive happen to the garden. Knowing that Nancy was moving to New York and looking for new projects, Vince asked him if he would introduce Nancy to the nuns at the facility. He did. Some three or four years later, she is still working on the project.

Vince recommended to Nancy that since Easter is a holiday during which families often visit patients, she plant someplace in the garden, or even in the cutting area in the nuns' part of the complex, different varieties of lilacs, some blooming earlier and some later, thus extending the season of bloom to more than two weeks. Actually, by using lilac bushes in conjunction with other plants, the period of bloom could be extended to six weeks or longer. The idea was that when people started to arrive, there would be fragrance in the foyer, which would rekindle memories for both the patients and their families. Although much work remains to be done, the process has begun. Nancy has already planted the first of the lilacs in the garden.

If there are bouquets of flowers where it is appropriate, where people are not going to be sickened by them, and if the fragrances are *familiar*, they are very likely to facilitate communication. This can be very important, he said. Elizabeth Kubler-Ross has pointed out that often family members come rushing in on patients, especially those in nursing homes, and put demands on them that they be other than what they are, rather than just walking in and quietly inviting them to *come back*. Often what happens is that the demands are what push the patients farther away, because of the *expectations*. Fragrances that rekindle family memories can bring both patients and their families to a mutually agreeable place.

In talking about the healing qualities of gardens in general, Vince tells another story about a friend in Los Angeles who was the wife of a landscape architect considered by Vince to be the most scholarly landscape architect of his generation. Several years after the architect's death, his widow (Vince's friend) was diagnosed with Alzheimer's disease. The woman's favorite place to be was in the garden designed by her husband. There was something about the garden that was so *forgiving* that it brought her back, even as the disease process continued its deterioration of her faculties. The garden was laid out in such a way that somehow, fortuitously, it was an ideal garden for this woman, because she could walk around in it virtually unattended. The pathways were set up such that they all looped. The woman could stroll wherever she wanted to. It was as if everything was set to accommodate the dementia as it came into play, as if the garden had been designed for someone with Alzheimer's as we understand it today. When the woman was with her family in the garden, there was a marked improvement from her interactions with them in the house.

Why is it that a garden design such as this, with pathways that loop, is somehow more effective than other designs? Is it the simplicity of the layout or the familiarity of the place? Vince believes that it is both these things, but that the mechanism is more complex. In explaining this, Vince distinguishes between *complicated* and *complex*. He notes that *complicated* is a Rube Goldberg machine so old that all 8000 pieces are breaking down at the same time. In contrast, *complex* is where although a lot is going on, it works so well together that one takes the process for granted.

On this occasion I asked Vince if the healing nature of that design is a sort of paradox, that is, having a *complex-simplicity*, which I believed I had discovered in studying the works of Alexander, Lynch, and Appleton. He responded that it is a paradox in some ways, but that in other ways it is not, in that it has to do with the successful integration and interrelationship of process to the point where it seems so simple that you take it for granted. By way of explanation, he went on to say that a safety pin is a very complex device when you take into consideration the fact that you have to have both the right alloy and the appropriate design to create the right spring effect. Yet, when you look at it, it is a very simple device. "My grandmother knew the guy who invented the safety pin," he said. "He called himself the 'Safety Pin King.' However, he became greatly humbled by a trip to Pompei, where he saw an ancient safety pin in the museum! The concept was very complex in certain ways, and yet, once you've got it, *it's there*! Once you've got it, you take it for granted. Often what appears simple isn't."

In discussing the complexity of the Los Angeles garden mentioned, Vince was of the opinion that the result appeared simple, in terms of offering places where the sun could shine through and taking into account that during the course of the year the relative position of the sun changed. But Vince felt that it took an enormous amount of extraordinarily complex thought processes to make it all work. The garden was built with the house, carved into the hillside and nestled in a wooded lot. The landscape architect had built the house and garden with his own two hands over a period of nearly 30 years. There had been a great deal of trial and error in the process.

In fact, Vince believes that it is precisely this long-term process of trial and error that makes the place so impressive. For him, the beauty of a garden is that you can treat it as a kind of living moquette that is constantly changing, where you can start with less expensive materials and sort of overlay more expensive materials as you progress. As you do this, you will eventually have a sense of what is supposed to be happening—and a complete composition that works well in its entirety.

Acknowledgments

Thanks are due to the personnel of The Family Life Center, Grand Rapids, MI; Hearthstone Alzheimer Care, Lexington, MA; The Champaign County Nursing Home, Urbana, IL; Milwaukee Jewish Home and Care Center-Helen Bader Center, Milwaukee, WI; Lodi Good Samaritan Center, Lodi, WI, and The Hawks Nursery Company, Wauwatosa, WI.

The Champaign County Nursing Home, Urbana, IL, kindly allowed me to use photographs of the Home's residents.

Special thanks go to Robert Leathers of Leathers and Associates, Inc., Ithaca, NY for use of his five-step community build concept; to Daniel Sjordal for his many wonderful illustrations; and to Paul Mayhew for his input on the process of design-build construction methods.

The
HEALING
LANDSCAPE

Introduction

The path that led me to undertaking this work was a personal and professional desire to grow in knowledge and understanding of designing appropriate and enjoyable outdoor spaces for people in need of physical, emotional, or spiritual healing. Along this path I encountered the work of many people: my ancestors, grandparents, family, friends, professors and classmates, practitioners, horticulturists, therapists, and gardeners. I soon discovered the simple truth that the landscape surrounding us has a great impact on our sense of well-being (Clemence, 1988; Cooper Marcus, 1978; Jensen, 1939; Tuan, 1980; Tyson, 1986, 1987). This led to a search for answers to the question, Why are gardens and gardening unique avenues of healing? Horticulturists and researchers had already plowed furrows that I had only to walk beside and study to begin to understand the world of horticultural therapy and the restorative qualities of nature (AHTA, 1988; Kaplan, 1973; Kaplan and Kaplan, 1996; Rothert and Daubert, 1981).

The not-so-logical progression of this path led me back to the principles of design and planning (Alexander et al., 1977; Appleton, 1996; Lynch, 1960) and back to the university to further study the psychology of human behavior and design. The introduction to the established and current work of researchers, professors, and practitioners led me to the discovery of the narrow gate that opened onto an ever-expanding avenue of people and resources in the field of environment-behavior studies (Anthony, 1990; Carstens, 1985; Cohen and Weisman, 1991; Weidemann et al., 1982; Zeisel, 1981).

The progression of knowledge and the practitioner within me led me to search for answers to the question, How can the theory be translated into reality, that is, into built landscapes? (Tyson, 1989, 1990, 1992). Any designer will quickly tell you that for each design problem there are as many solutions as minds working to solve it. Therefore, one logical and

Walking alongside the furrows.

The garden gate.

"What is essential is invisible to the eye"
(Saint-Exupéry, 1943).

practical research response is to design a study in which results take form as a list of guidelines from which designers can draw on the experience of past practice and research (Carey, 1986; Carpman, Grant, and Simmons, 1986; Cooper Marcus and Francis, 1990). The dynamic nature of the garden often goes beyond the categories of guidelines, involving people in the process of creating and tending to the ongoing life of the garden itself. Researchers and practitioners are beginning to create bridges in the restorative garden-nature arena to confirm and expand the existing knowledge base of how interaction (whether passive or active) with nature affects the well-being of people. The introduction of this work to students, professionals, health care providers, and the general public has opened many new paths for research and practice (Betrabet, G. 1997; Cooper Marcus and Barnes, 1995; Cooper Marcus and Francis, 1990; Dannenmaer, 1995; Healy, 1991; Hester and Francis, 1990; Kamp, 1996; Relph, 1992; Rothert, 1994; Warner, 1994) that will lead to new paths just around the next bend.

I have not created a set of guidelines or prescriptive method of developing a garden, but rather a way of thought, that is, a process of solving problems, providing a pathway to follow and ideas to interpret and distill. First we try to distinguish the intrinsic qualities of a garden and then to establish the therapeutic milieu or spiritual and material benefits to people who come in contact with the garden. We will place our focus on people—people in the garden, the atmosphere created, the lively interaction of people tending to plants and resting in and pondering the beauty and *complex simplicity* of nature. Here we will find the path to restoring the soul, capturing the imagination, clearing the mind, illuminating the senses, and healing the body.

On these pages we will follow the path of my search for meaning in ordinary life—in nature, in human behavior, in design, in the art of composing a living tapestry of plants and people for the purpose of healing:

"Goodbye," said the fox. "And now here is my secret, a very simple secret: It is only with the heart that one can see rightly; what is essential is invisible to the eye." "What is essential is invisible to the eye," the Little Prince repeated, so that he would be sure to remember. "It is the time that you have devoted to your rose that makes your rose so important." "It is the time I have devoted to my rose—" said the Little Prince, so that he would be sure to remember. "Men have forgotten this truth," said the fox. "But you must not forget it. You become responsible, forever, for what you have tamed. You are responsible for your rose." "I am responsible for my rose," the Little Prince repeated, so that he would be sure to remember (Saint-Exupéry, 1943, p. 70).

We will look at the garden in the context of the individual and of the larger social dimension. In an age in which efficiency and immediate gains or profit are emphasized, there lies the possibility of reducing the worth of the individual to his or her ability to contribute materially to society, as opposed to seeing the intrinsic value of each as a human person regardless of age or ability. This may greatly affect more vulnerable individuals in society, including the elderly, disabled, and those with declining health.

Often there are no known cures for an illness or disability. In addition, individuals may at times appear to be unaware of their surroundings and seem unresponsive to what many consider to be quality living experiences. With limited understanding of the internal world of people who suffer from diseases and disabilities of the mind, care must be taken to provide familiar and comfortable settings to assure the highest quality of living experience possible for these individuals and their care-givers.

Health care providers, family members, and design professionals are challenged with designing and building specialized living environments and developing social programming to provide comfort and dignity resulting in a better quality of daily life. There is no formula for creating the perfect environment. Current research and historic examples show that a homelike atmosphere designed to encourage participation with ordinary daily domestic activities may be especially therapeutic for people in a vulnerable state of mind or physical health (Bailey et al., 1961; Cohen and Weisman, 1991; Dowling, 1995; Healy, 1997; Mace, 1993; U.S. Department of Health and Human Services, 1992).

The garden or landscape is connected to people in a way that is uniquely healing in its essence. The restorative qualities of gardens span the human spectrum and have no social, cultural, or ethnic boundaries. Gardens may contain elements that are specific to culture, climate, or time; however, the simple truth of their existence reflects the universal desire for human interaction with nature, with humans as the stewards of the land.

Restorative Qualities of Gardens

Historically, healing gardens were places designed for the restoration of the mind, soul, and body. During the Middle Ages, monastery courtyards served as places for contemplation, for growing vegetables, fruit, herbs for medicinal purposes, and flowers such as roses, lilies, and iris for ceremonial use (Berrall, 1966). The cloistered gardens provided respite for infirm monks and weary travelers as well as serving meditative and agrarian purposes (Berrall, 1966; Von Miklos and Fiore, 1968). Monastic documents show that within the enclosure of the monastery walls, there were several distinct garden types. In some orders where monks lived as hermits in silence, each lived in a separate cell around

A cloister garden.

the cloister with a small walled garden attached to it. Believed to be the most common type of monastery garden of medieval western Europe, the central cloister planted with turf was kept green not only to symbolize rebirth and everlasting life but to refresh the eyes and minds of the monks as they spent much of their time inside the darkness of the monastery. Often one cloister garden had a juniper planted in the corner to symbolize the tree of life, and others were in a cruciform pattern creating four quadrangles with a central well or fountain (Landsberg, 1995; Warner, 1994).

A document believed to have been created by a monk in the early part of the ninth century describes a plan of an ideal garden for the Benedictine Monastery of Saint Gall in Switzerland, although the garden may never have actually been built (King, 1979). Shown on the plan are the *cloister garth* (an open quadrangle with intersecting paths for the monks to walk in the fresh air), a well or fountain (usually found in the center of the courtyard), cemetery orchard, herb garden, green court, kitchen court, and infirmary garden. Outside the cloister walls there were the *cellarer's garden,* several acres of crops to supply necessary food for workers, visitors, and the poor, and the *peasant closes,* small utilitarian gardens adjacent to village homesteads (Landsberg, 1995). A well-known ancient Swedish garden legend speaks of the miracle of the "Christmas Rose," in which an aged abbot is led to a garden known to bloom deep in the forest every Christmas Eve, and the little white flower continues to "rise miraculously from the cold wintry earth, serving to remind us that life is full of miracles" (Greene, 1990).

Some of the greatest mystics of Christianity speak of the garden as a place of union with their God, often using flowers, trees, and elements of the natural world in their expressions of prayer. Saint John of the Cross often wrote prose describing his spiritual life in terms of the beauty of nature: "I find in my Beloved the mountains, the lonely and wooded vales, the distant isles, the murmur of the waters, the soft whisper of the zephyrs" (Taylor, 1927, p. 379). Saint Thérèse of Lisieux, known to the faithful as "The Little Flower," was influenced by memories of her childhood home in France; named "Le Pavillion," this small home was set at the gates of the town "in the midst of a large garden, full of flowers and fruit trees" (Morteveille, 1942, p. 14). Her writings describe her "little way" to heaven: "The little child will strew flowers…and she [the church] will smile on her little child and gather up the petals of these roses; placing them in your divine hands that they may acquire an infinite value" (Morteveille, 1942, p. 254).

A shower of roses (Christopher Miracle).

The Church itself was instrumental in the establishment of hospitals during the Middle Ages that have made an impact on the delivery of health care through the centuries. The legend of Irish-born "Lily of Eire" Saint Dympna, believed to have been martyred by her insane father, led to the establishment of a colony of mental patients whose families came to Gheel, Belgium, on pilgrimage to the site of Saint Martin's Chapel in search of healing from mental illness and nervous disorders (Wedge, 1996). The original precedent for care remains as an exceptionally humane model of community-based care for the mentally ill (Van Ravensteyn,1995). In his research of the history of hospital gardens, Sam Bass Warner notes that during the late Middle Ages the religious connection between spiritual healing and the garden began to fade and give way to a more humanistic view of medicine. As hospitals developed, the cloistered garden often was replaced by an open area for patients to walk and take in the sunshine and fresh air. Some progressive hospitals that primarily cared for people with mental illness placed a greater emphasis on the active work of tending to gardens and fields. For example; In fifteenth-century Spain at the Hospital at Zaragossa, a routine of normal daily activities including gardening was encouraged for patients rather than confining them as was the custom at the time (Warner, 1994). Florence Nightingale, the founder of the modern profession of nursing, stresses the importance of fresh air and natural sunlight on the well-being and healing of patients in her manual *Notes on Nursing* (Nightingale, 1873). Tracing the history of gardens shows us that there is a common thread of belief in the importance of fresh air, sunshine, access to nature, and working the land in the healing process (Warner, 1994).

Access to a positive outdoor area can add a new dimension to the total care program and can have a profound effect on patients, visitors,

Filling the birdbath.

and staff. A coordinated effort to design buildings and landscapes to work in harmony can also facilitate interaction by creating inviting outdoor places that draw people's interest and encourage use of the outdoors or observation from indoors. This interaction is the instrument that acts as the catalyst for both physical and spiritual healing (Cooper Marcus and Barnes, 1995; Kaplan and Kaplan, 1990; Landsberg, 1990; Lewis, 1990; Paine and Francis, 1990; Stoneham, 1990; Ulrich, 1984,1992; Uzzel and Lewand, 1990).

When planning and designing outdoor spaces for restorative purposes, it is critical to realize that often it is the little things that can make a big difference. The illustration, by history, of the importance of the garden clearly tells us that it is possible that within the ordinary life and circumstances are hidden many profound events of life. "It is because they are so ordinary, indeed, that they strike to the core" (Alexander et al., 1979, p. 219).

It is in this spirit that the garden begins to take form to bring its simplicity and sense of hope into the lives of many people in need of healing. The familiar smell and sight of lilacs or roses, the taste of a fresh tomato from the vine, or the feel of smooth leaves from an oak tree or soil warmed from the sun are experiences that only the garden can provide. With a vision of the therapeutic potential of landscape design as an integral part of the care program, the following chapters present a process for creating bridges between people through common experiences in the garden.

The Process

Understanding the philosophy and direction of the process is the beginning of the pathway to the creation of healing landscapes. Following this path will bring meaning and life to an otherwise traditional and often static process of design and construction. The communication of the process to key advisors to the garden project is essential to begin the pathway of the project. In some cases, the patterns of design are "somehow alive and help people give life to their surroundings"; however, "the mere use of patterns alone does not ensure that people can make places live" (Alexander et al., 1977, p. 229). The process lives through the people who are invested and help to create the place and give it meaning and life.

According to *Webster's Dictionary*, a *landscape* is defined as "A portion of territory that the eye can comprehend in a single view." A *yard* is defined as "A small usually walled and often paved area open to the sky and adjacent to a building." A *garden* is defined as "**1a:** a plot of ground where herbs, fruits, flowers or vegetables are cultivated. **b:** a rich well-cultivated region. **c:** a container (as a window box) planted with usually a

Lively solitude in the garden (Daniel Sjordal).

variety of small plants. **2a**: a public recreation area or park. **b**: an open-air drinking or eating place" (Morris, 1981).

What makes a *healing garden* different from any other garden? Are not all gardens and landscapes in some way healing to those who use them? This question is increasingly on the minds of design professionals and health care providers as the concept of therapeutic and healing environments becomes more integrated into the discussion of health care facility design.

The common foundation is in the simple truth that as human beings, we are in fact part of the larger created natural world; therefore, we can assert that we are designed to live in harmony with this world of nature.

This work is based on principles of design, of human behavior, and of the investment of people in the creation of their environment.

The process, the path of travel, is what gives the landscapes meaning, form, order, and life.

We begin with an understanding of the people, their history, abilities, and social patterns. We discover the meaning of gardens for the people who will live, work, or visit the garden and facility we are designing. Each

We are born into this world of nature.

The joy of ordinary work in the garden (Alicia Flynn).

We invest ourselves and watch them grow.

A garden is ageless in wisdom and simplicity.

A quiet place to rest and dream.

The Cloisters (New York City).

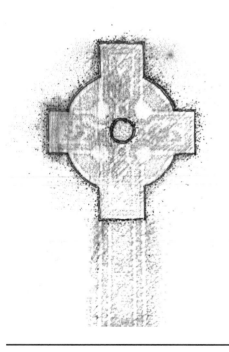

Complex simplicity gives form and order.

designed project is unique. The type of facility and therapeutic programs may determine design elements based on specific needs of patients and/or residents and staff. Conditions will vary. Local customs and architectural style, climate and plant material, as well as the social and physical context in which the facility is set, will have an impact on the design solution. The goal is to provide the tools necessary to assist people in the process of planning, designing, and building a garden.

Perceptions of gardens may vary from a warm and sunny place to a cool and shady place, a sanctuary for birds, a place where you plant and work the soil, or perhaps a place of solitude and contemplation. These images are formed from memories of places encountered as travelers, neighbors, children, gardeners, and observers throughout our lives. People respond to gardens or natural scenes in different ways. The manner in which people interact either actively or passively with the outdoor area affects the individual therapeutic outcome of the experience. An outdoor area may be designed to invite visiting and active participation. A view from a window of the garden may invite observation and calm reflection. Our objective is to explore principles of design theory and apply behavioral research methods to produce therapeutic goals and a language of design patterns that when thoughtfully composed, will result in designs that offer positive therapeutic benefits to patients, staff, and visitors.

To renew the sense of historic precedent, the process is laid out in the form of the cloister garden. The four quadrants represent the four parts of the process, and the central well represents the philosophy of the garden as a place of healing.

The first part of the process describes the methods of investigation suggested to establish therapeutic goals for the people who will use the garden.

The second part describes the formulation of a language of design patterns, that is, the process of developing concepts and composing the final plan from which to build the garden.

The third part describes how to successfully involve people in the process as a way of building the project that requires the investment of people.

The fourth part describes the process of evaluating the garden and program, introducing an active therapeutic dimension, and suggesting future paths for design and research.

The process is not laid out to be followed as a prescriptive method but rather, as a point of departure for creating designs and conducting research according to the specific needs and intentions of each project. The concepts, however, are rooted in the theories of the science of human behavior and design principles. In this way, the path provides a strong foundation for planning, designing, building, and using gardens that are designed to bring the restorative qualities of the landscape into the lives of those who are in need of physical, emotional, and spiritual healing.

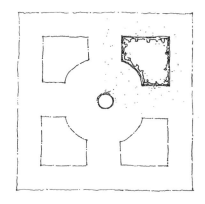

Quadrant 1: Investigate.

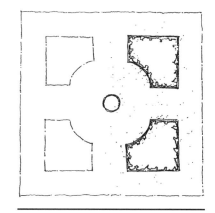

Quadrant 2 : Design.

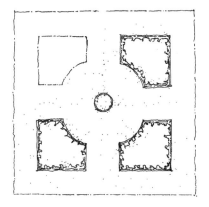

Quadrant 3: Build.

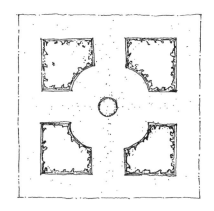

Quadrant 4: Evaluate.

A gateway to new paths.

Investigate

CHAPTER 1

Conduct Behavioral Research

For every design problem, there is a process that leads to a solution or series of solutions. However formal or informal the methods of gathering information, the preliminary stage requires evaluating the site and user needs. In the traditional design process, emphasis is placed on the inventory and analysis of site conditions, landscape features, and architectural form. Designs are often completed with limited knowledge of the actual people who will be using the outdoor area.

In assessing the future of the profession of landscape architecture, Lane Marshall, author of *Action by Design* (1983), stresses responsible design and the importance of integrated efforts between design and user needs, although he recognizes the fact that behavioral research methods are seldom applied: "Few design clients demand their use, and fewer still are sensitive to their value. If quality of life is to be our ultimate goal, however, we must incorporate these techniques in the design decision-making process." An example is given of the Pruitt-Igoe low-income housing project built in St. Louis in the 1950s. The design earned numerous architectural awards but totally disregarded the needs of residents. The design philosophy suggested that people would adapt to buildings which were attractive. As a result, the housing project eventually became "a menace to human life." The structure was demolished fewer than 20 years after construction (Marshall, 1983, p.117). Environmental psychology researchers in housing, architecture, and urban planning have since conducted investigative studies of perceptions of people living in similar housing settings. The results have made considerable impact on the public housing industry, suggesting improvements in design and management of similar public housing projects (Weidemann et al., 1982).

When designing *therapeutic* environments, determining the behavioral relationship between the physical surroundings and the people who use them is even more critical. Environmental psychology is a relatively new discipline that specifically addresses the impact of the environment on psychological well-being. "We know from research, for example, that design can enhance the therapeutic process, by improving the recovery rate of patients in hospitals. More research is therefore needed to understand the psychological consequences and benefits of landscape design for particular groups of people in particular environments" (Uzzel and Lewand, 1990, p. 34). Current research is beginning to search for the underlying explanations of how the landscape does affect the well-being of people who come into contact with nature (further discussed in Chap. 4).

What constitutes an appropriate outdoor environment for varied medical impairments or psychological conditions is a complex issue. The primary focus of design should, however, be to meet the needs of the people using the space while developing the full therapeutic potential of the outdoor space or garden.

Issues for Evaluating or Preparing a Program of Use

There are three basic issues to address in evaluating an existing facility or preparing the program for a new facility design. The first is determining how residents' physical, emotional, cognitive, and social functioning and life satisfaction have been improved or maintained by design or programming. The second is determining the impact of the design on residents, family, and staff, and the third is determining the costs involved in building and maintaining the design (U.S. DHHS, NIH, 1992).

Design Interventions

The physical environment is one of multiple factors considered in defining the overall quality of services delivered in health care settings (Cooper Marcus and Barnes, 1995; U.S. DHHS, NIH, 1983). Modification of the physical environment is preferred to medication in the treatment of most behavioral problems (APA, DSM-IV, 1994; Post, 1992). Design interventions that focus on behavioral issues may be one way to improve the quality of care and environment. Concepts for design modifications to assist in the intervention of problem behaviors are most effective if they are usable for both staff who care for people in health care settings and family members who care for their loved one at home. Research and design projects in landscape architecture cover a broad spectrum includ-

Building bridges between research and design.

ing housing for disabled and elderly, hospital garden design, children's environments, community gardens, and gardens designed specifically for people with AIDS or Alzheimer's disease (i.e., Butterfield, 1982; Carstens, 1985, 1990; Goltsman et al., 1990; Hester and Francis, 1990; Kamp, 1996; Mooney and Nicell, 1992; Moore et al., 1992; Paine and Francis, 1990; Stoneham and Thoday, 1996; Tyson, 1992). Using the modern design process, a practicing design professional who wants to take advantage of research available is often confronted with barriers and gaps in the communication of information. As a result, often designs fall short of their full potential by limited response to user needs.

John Zeisel, sociologist and author of *Inquiry by Design: Tools for Environment-Behavior Research* (1981), addresses the issue of overcoming barriers and bridging gaps; "E-B [environment-behavior] research changes the boundary by making more visible to designers the needs, desires and reactions of users to their surroundings, thus enabling designers to better negotiate with users and understand the effects of decisions on them" (Zeisel, 1981, p. 35).

Environmental design researchers study the range of relationships between people and their environment (physical, social, and cultural). Application of this research can impact environmental policy, programming, and design (University of Wisconsin, 1997). Opportunities for the cooperative association of research and design include developing a *program of user needs*, which describes the intent of the built garden, *design review*, and *evaluation* of built projects in use (Zeisel, 1981, pp. 35–36). Although a designer may not have the benefit of working directly with the client-users, there are other means of gaining user-based information. You can gather information from research conducted elsewhere or conduct case study research with a similar group of people (Zeisel, 1981, p. 38).

Case studies that evaluate existing projects will provide recommendations for design criteria based on research or practical experience in landscape architecture and allied professions. Reviewing case studies or postoccupancy evaluations of existing facilities that document detailed

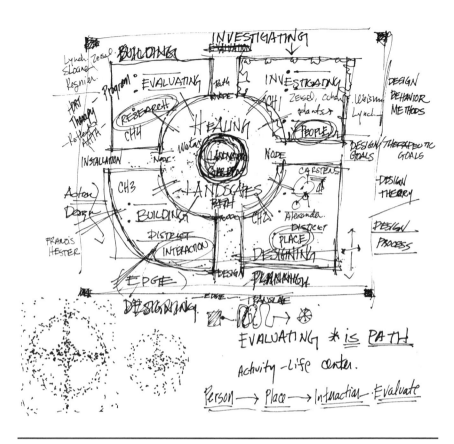

The evolution of the process.

descriptions of the sites, that is, the outdoor spaces and how they are used, will help in the development of plans for programming and design. Understanding successful features and unsuccessful features will provide valuable insight for design. These features are often categorized, which facilitates choosing those that may be most suitable for future postoccupancy evaluations, designs, or research (Cooper Marcus and Francis, 1990).

Instruments including checklists, questionnaires, or rating scales for assessing behavioral problems and for recording observations of how people interact with the physical environment or perceptions of surroundings are available in published research reports (Carpman et al., 1986; Cooper Marcus and Francis, 1990; Goltsman et al., 1992; Mooney and Nicell, 1992; Sloane and Matthew, 1990; Weidemann et al., 1982; Zeisel et al., 1994).

Literature Search

Searching for information ranges from an informal inquiry for most practitioners to an in-depth structured research literature survey for a team of researchers in a particular field. In either case, it is desirable to have a clear set of questions to assure that the information is relevant to the desired end result (i.e., a built project, case study, evaluation, or basic research). Literature searches or reviews involve networking to discover relevant information on the topic and related topics (i.e., health care design or therapeutic alternatives). Sources to begin a search for these project reports include but are not limited to *Environment and Behavior*, *Landscape Design* (UK), *Landscape Journal* and *Landscape Research* (UK) as well as conference proceedings and in-house publications from the International Association for the Study of People and their Physical Environment (IAPS), People and Physical Environment Research (PAPER), the Environmental Design Research Association (EDRA), American Institute of Architects (AIA), American Society of Landscape Architects (ASLA), American Horticultural Therapy Association (AHTA), Horticulture Therapy (UK), and some recently founded health care–design advocacy groups (i.e., Center for Health Design, Inc., Planetree International, Healing Healthcare Network, and People-Plant Network).

The methods of searching information are constantly being updated or improved depending on the most current technological advances. Computerized methods of searching are available via the Internet and the World Wide Web and the vast available online library connections. It is still valid, however, to conduct an old-fashioned but often more interesting search method: wandering the stacks and library shelves to find other related books (books on similar subjects are usually grouped together). Another direct and equally effective method of expanding your search is contacting representatives of local or nationwide health care agencies working with the specific populations for whom you are designing. These additional sources will open doors to many helpful avenues of assistance. It is a challenge, while on your quest for knowledge, to discern whether information is reliable and relevant to your particular project needs (Sommer and Sommer, 1986). The amount of information can be overwhelming to both beginning researchers and those with advanced experience; therefore, enlisting the assistance of library-science professionals or staff of university research departments is recommended.

Research Systems

The type of research study suggests the appropriate system of collecting data. Methodology depends on the intended use or application of the information. For practical application to projects being constructed, an appropriate research study type may be *action research*, which "combines the testing of theory with application." *Applied research* "seeks practical answers to immediate questions," yielding information that is applicable to other similar projects. *Instrumental research* is most commonly associated with academic work, the primary goal being to "demonstrate competence in research." *Basic research* "seeks answers to long-range questions" adding to the existing body of knowledge (Sommer and Sommer, 1986, p. 5).

Good research is both *valid* and *reliable.* A study is considered *valid* if the research tools or procedures actually measure and accomplish what they were set up to (*internal validity*) and are able to be applied to similar settings or situations (*external validity*). *Reliability* is tested by the application of instruments and procedures to similar projects to obtain equally significant results (Sommer and Sommer, 1986). Research conducted in *natural settings* (those not created for the purpose of research experiments) is considered to be more successful at obtaining real-life information that can be applied to a more generalized set of situations. This ability to generalize the information, referred to as *external validity*, makes the natural setting more appealing to those engaged in action or applied research studies (Kidder and Judd, 1986; Sommer and Sommer, 1986; Zeisel, 1981).

The research conducted in the allied design professions is either applied or action research when the results are to be applied to built environments, as is the goal of design-behavior research in the *creation* of healing outdoor environments. It is recommended that a multimethod approach be taken to increase the validity of research. Of the many research designs, the most appropriate to our purposes include (1) observation, (2) case study, (3) quasi-experiment, and (4) survey.

1. *Observation* has a twofold purpose of collecting and recording information. The first is the systematic recording of existing patterns of use through the study of physical traces or "detective" work. Observing physical traces is somewhat akin to archeology in that the researcher makes note of signs of use or alteration of the environment by people who have been there (i.e., shortcut paths worn in lawn areas, movement of furnishings, or graffiti). The second is the systematic observation of people and how they use settings, what they do and how it is affected by the layout of the physical environment.

At first glance, behavior observation may seem like little more than advanced people watching. To obtain usable results, however, some form of systematic record keeping needs to be in place. When undertaking the task of conducting observations at a particular site, you should first decide what you are looking for and then how to record the information (Zeisel, 1981). Informal observation techniques include field notes and sketches to describe what is happening during your observation time.

A more systematic approach to observation involves some predetermined criteria. The study must have a specified research purpose—for example, to determine walking paths and destinations of elderly residents in a courtyard.

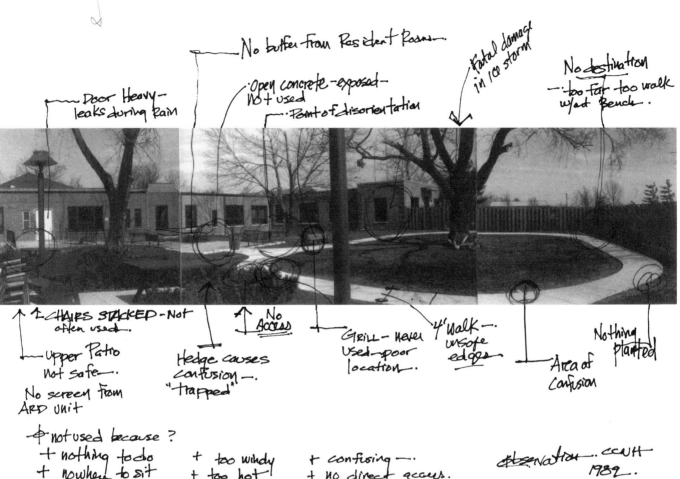

Observations of behavior traces.

The observations must be planned systematically by developing a schedule of timed intervals for observations and a checklist of behaviors to observe. The study observations must be recorded systematically on a precoded list and base map of the courtyard. Following the series of observation sessions, the information gathered will need to be compiled, analyzed, and documented for the research report. There are two methods of communicating the collected information: developing an annotated plan showing the intended or actual uses of existing areas and a written design review based on performance program that is a way of testing the design (Zeisel, 1981, p. 43).

2. A *case study* is similar to historical research in that it is written and reconstructed after the event has taken place or the place is in use. The advantage of the case study is in its attention to detail and its in-depth look at a particular situation. Researchers choose a case study model when they want specific information about a particular group of people in particular settings (i.e., therapeutic benefits of hospital gar-

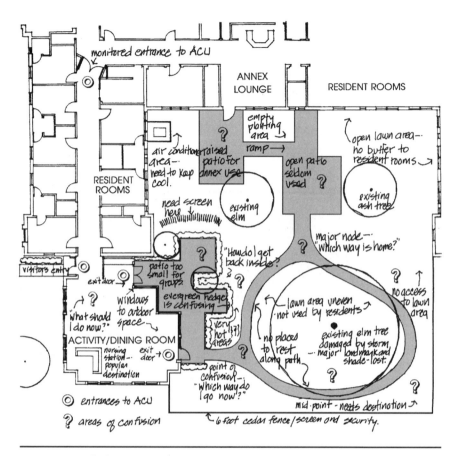

An annotated plan documenting patterns of use.

dens, housing options for the mentally ill and disabled, or positive effects of community garden programs). A good example of this type of research is Cooper Marcus and Francis, *People Places*, 1990. Although in theory limited to individual sites and situations, it is possible to develop "generalizable" models that can be applied to other settings, such as "when case studies are carried out on topics which have been studied before and about which some theory exists…or…choosing a setting that is in many ways typical of other settings" (Zeisel, 1981, p. 67). In this way, research from allied professions or other disciplines within landscape architecture can be built upon and improve the foundation of research knowledge.

3. The **quasi-experiment** is a research design that studies the before and after effects of some change in the environment. It differs from a true scientific experiment because it is conducted outside of a controlled laboratory setting (Campbell and Stanley, 1963). The design is most effective when used as a *pretest-posttest* (observing behavior or perceptions before and after some intentional change in the physical surroundings) or a *static-group comparison* (comparing the perceptions or behavior of two similar groups of people within different settings)

[Kidder and Judd, 1986]. This is a valuable tool for evaluating the use of a particular outdoor area to determine its therapeutic benefit to users.

4. The *survey design* may include interviews, questionnaires, or attitude and rating scales. Depending on the purpose of gathering information, you may choose to use one or more of the methods. Interviews are valued for obtaining specific information on feelings and attitudes of people on a particular subject. An interview can be formally structured or loosely structured depending on the situation and application of information obtained. For example, an interview with front-line staff in an intensive care unit during the normal routine of the day will require a predetermined, concise, clear set of questions that can be answered in a short period of time with room for interruptions. An interview with patients on a psychiatric ward may require the interviewer to be flexible with a loosely formulated set of questions and to allot more time for the session. A *focused interview* is another tool used with either small groups or individuals to obtain in-depth information and perceptions in a "particular concrete situation," for example, patients in the same hospital, residents of the same housing complex, or working in the same health care setting (Zeisel, 1981, p. 139).

Questionnaire

The use of questionnaires is the most economical method of obtaining information from a large group of people, although return rates vary considerably. A questionnaire requires a well-defined problem and careful organization of questions. Experienced researchers often use questionnaires to test and refine previous research; for example, in low-income housing projects, residents may be asked to answer questions about perceived safety and satisfaction with their home environment (Weidemann et al., 1982). Unlike more subjective methods, a questionnaire can provide results that can be analyzed and quantified accurately manually or with the help of statistical analysis computer programs to produce results in an objective measurable format. The value of the questionnaire is that the researcher can compare the responses, identifying perceptions and attitudes, to the same set of questions. The questions themselves require attention to wording, sequence of inquiries, and coding procedures to be certain that data are usable and able to be analyzed with statistical measures. For example, a sample question may be, Does your hospital have windows in rooms? Yes or No. A follow-up question may be, If yes, what are the views from the windows? Depending on the desired results, the researcher may choose to leave a blank line for the respondent to complete or a list of possible scenes to choose from (e.g., landscape scene, parking lot, hospital service entry, solid wall, or surrounding neighborhood).

2. Do you notice that residents who wander seem to follow a pattern?

   ✔ yes ☐ no ☐ not sure

3. Please sketch your observed pattern below, noting possible destinations.

4. How often are you able to identify the following as destinations?

	very often			never		N/A
window to outdoors	✔	☐	☐	☐	☐	☐
exit door to outdoors	✔	☐	☐	☐	☐	☐

other, please specify _Street —. Neighbors —._

Restlessness/Agitation

3. When residents become restless or anxious, how frequently do you do the following?

	very often			never		N/A
walking with resident indoors	✔	☐	☐	☐	☐	☐
walking with resident outdoors	☐	☐	✔	☐	☐	☐
physical restraint	☐	☐	☐	✔	☐	☐
medication	☐	☐	☐	☐	✔	☐

other, please specify _talking —_

Windows and Views Outdoors

3. How often do you notice *weather* changes affecting patient mood/behavior?

very often	frequently	sometimes	rarely	never
☐	✔	☐	☐	☐

4. Describe characteristic behaviors when residents are affected by *weather changes*?

Agitation when storms come —. less agitated with weather that they can go outdoors. If door is locked. More agitated and difficult to deal with —. Not secured —.

Questions of observation and interaction.

The organization and order of the questions will usually flow from factual information to more specific or controversial questions later in the questionnaire (Sommer and Sommer, 1986). A questionnaire can include additional means of gathering information like attitude rating scales. An example of an attitude rating scale question is, How often do residents look out the window? *Very often∗Often∗Sometimes∗Almost never∗Never.* The respondent is asked to give an answer within the range of choices. A follow-up scale may be, How important do you feel a window view to a natural scene is for patient well-being? *Very important∗Important∗Somewhat important∗Not very important∗Not at all important* (Kidder and Judd, 1986).

Part of the questionnaire may require visual responses to drawings or architectural plans or photographs—for example, if you are inquiring about current patterns of use of an existing hospital courtyard, the researcher may include a scaled drawing of the space and ask respondents to trace their usual path from indoors through the courtyard. Information gathered from visual response questions is valuable for design-behavior researchers to analyze and evaluate existing projects. In some cases, it is appropriate to request respondents to draw a sketch or map describing a place they have been or would imagine as a design solution for a proposed project (Zeisel, 1981); however, my personal experience suggests an unexplained universal aversion to drawing, which often limits illustrated responses. Questionnaires require patient review and revision by consultants experienced in the design, layout, wording, and organization of material and analysis. After several stages of testing, however, using the tool is a valuable way of conducting research (Sommer and Sommer, 1986).

The questions on page 22 are from a questionnaire directed to front-line staff at Alzheimer's Care Centers as part of a research study at the University of Illinois at Urbana-Champaign (Tyson et al.,1990). The first is a question about resident behavior, followed by visual response request and rating scale.

Identify Primary Users and Project Site

Identifying People Who Will Use the Garden

To develop a plan that responds to the activities and life of people who will eventually use the outdoor areas, it is important to identify those people. You will need to gather information about the residents, staff, and family, as well as information about the existing site conditions. You will be more successful during the design phase of the process if your analysis of users is thorough. At this point you should think of everyone that may use the outdoor area—for example, residents, staff, family, visitors, gardeners, maintenance staff, activities staff, nurses, aides, volunteers, and administrators. Administration will have specific needs related to quality of care, budget concerns, general operations and management. Finally, the needs and desires of family and visitors will also affect the design.

The benefits of collaborative efforts are an integral part of the overall therapeutic program of the garden. The investment of people in the project gives the design and continued growth of the garden a human and spiritual dimension by which the garden possesses a sense of liveliness or life. The modern practice of construction unfortunately often leaves out the dimension of participation that is so essential to the continued life of the place and people.

This preliminary work will not always present its benefits at the outset; however, it can prevent the postconstruction discovery of design issues that may have been corrected early on in the process. The role of systematic information gathering is to help designers better understand how people relate to their surroundings, which will lead to more appropriate designs. Often, what is perceived as an attractive garden design, based on a designer's training and experience, may not be the most supportive or appropriate design for people with cognitive or physical impairments. This is usually a challenge for designers because it involves a transformation of mind and behavior to a completely new role and way of thinking (De Long, 1970). The way to "put yourself into another's shoes" is to learn as much as you can about him or her and apply that knowledge to the design.

Here is an example of a project illustrating this point, contributed by landscape architect Paul Mayhew, a colleague from Minnesota. A landscape architect was asked to design an outdoor waiting area for a dentist's office. The site was to offer some seating with plantings and a sculpture to help create a nice atmosphere. The site was also to have a walkway to take you from the office door to the seating area. People who would use the site would be staff and patients. The goal of the design was to provide a nice place to sit while waiting for the dentist. The landscape architect designed a small viewing garden, and it was installed. It had a walkway made out of square stepping pads with ground cover growing in between that led to a garden bench to sit on and view a garden sculpture, centered in a small shade garden.

When the project was complete, the dentist and his staff loved it. Two days later, however, they called the designer asking that he come out and redesign the walkway. It seems they had forgotten to mention that some of the patients using the new space have just undergone dental work that requires the use of nitrous oxide, and they needed to wait

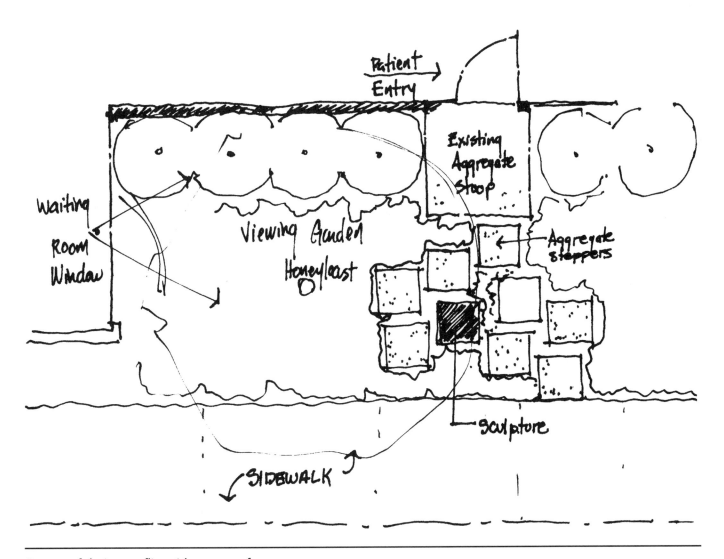

Pattern of design conflict with pattern of use.

15 or 20 minutes before they could leave. Because of the dizziness from the gas, when patients went out to use the new waiting area, they could not negotiate the spacing of the stepping pads in the walkway, creating a dangerous walk for patients.

The design was reworked, and a more direct walkway surface replaced the stepping stones, creating a more inviting and safe entrance. This may seem a very elemental design problem; however, it illustrates that a few preliminary questions or inquiries into the intended use is of great value in the design process from this small-scale site design to large-scale campus planning or institutional projects (Mayhew, 1997).

Function follows form.

Form follows function.

Defining Individual Needs

Some questions to help you identify the users and define their individual needs are provided for a starting point. First, you may want to define who will be using the space. Will it be designed for residents, staff, family and visitors, or people in the surrounding community? Then you may want to ask, for whom is the outdoor area *primarily* being designed? Will it be a space specifically for resident or patient use, or will it be available to all residents, staff, and visitors? The intent of gathering information about the people who will use the outdoor areas is to produce general criteria or guideposts to follow as you begin to forge your own path. It is important to identify who the primary users of the planned outdoor spaces will be in order to make an appropriate evaluation of site selection for the gardens.

Determining Characteristic Behaviors

There is no single description that can characterize all people, most particularly those who suffer from some physical or cognitive impairments, which includes most individuals in health care settings. Therefore it is critical to obtain direct information from staff trained to work in specific medical settings in addition to relevant research and literature. In educational and medical professions, labels are often used to describe characteristic behaviors associated with cognitive or physical conditions. Although common labels are used, each individual has distinctive behavioral characteristics.

Three commonly used labels to describe people with "special needs" include disorder, disability, and handicap. A *disorder* refers to a "general malfunction of mental, physical, or psychological processes" and is further defined as a "disturbance in normal functioning." A *disability* is the result of loss of some physical function or condition that "significantly interferes" with a person's ability to learn or perform in normal social situations and impedes "normal growth and development." A *handicap* is defined as a "limitation" imposed by the demands of the environment and directly responds to the individual's "ability to adapt or adjust to those demands." An example is given of a person using a wheelchair for mobility. This person has a physical disability—the inability to walk. When this person encounters physical barriers in a building or outdoor recreational setting, the disability becomes a handicap imposed by the environment (Hardman et al., 1993). Within the allied design fields, we have available a growing number of excellent resources for design solutions and guidelines that respond to physical disability, and some diseases of the mind. Understanding the behaviors associated with specific medical conditions, especially those connected with cognition, is a preliminary step to developing therapeutic goals for design. It is critical to understand the behavior patterns associated with a condition in order to create environments that support abilities and promote independence as much as possible. Usually rehabilitative changes occur gradually and vary among different people. To accommodate the different needs resulting from these changes, either the person must adapt to their surroundings or the physical environment must be altered.

People who have suffered some cognitive impairment often compensate for the sensory losses by developing an increased dependency on close proximity to each other and more direct dependence on the physical environment (De Long, 1970). Some people are able to adapt quite well; however, more complex issues like severe sensory loss or memory impairment may compound the problems encountered. Severe impairment of cognitive functioning and ability to negotiate and perceive the environment may result in people becoming even more dependent on their immediate surroundings for support. One successful way of managing or dealing with behavioral problems that may arise is to design the environment to help staff prevent these problems from occurring or escalating (Mace, 1993).

Appropriate patterns of intended use and design models are determined by evaluating existing facilities and ongoing research in environmental psychology and design. According to the research of city planning theorist Kevin Lynch, the way in which a person perceives the environment normally takes the form of developing an internal map or vignette of information to process location, path, and destination. When cognition is impaired, however, these internal processes are incomplete and may cause distress to the individual (Lynch, 1960). The power of memory is significant in the life of people who suffer from cognitive loss or severe brain trauma.

Thoughts, images, and responsive emotions that may have once been retrieved without a second thought often are confused or incomplete and sometimes lost forever. This can have a devastating effect on people suffering from the loss of memory as well as those people who support and care for them. Following the logic of this theory, if the actual physical layout is designed to minimize the risk of confusion, then a pathway experience can in fact change the perception of a more vulnerable person to ameliorate a catastrophic response. Depending on the level of severity and type of trauma, the cognitive response differs. Disorientation—that is, difficulty with spatial clarity and way finding—can be extremely distressing. "To become completely lost is perhaps a rather rare experience for most people, in the modern city (maps, way finding, signs, street numbers, etc.)....But let the mishap of disorientation once occur, and the sense of anxiety and even terror that accompanies it reveals to us how closely it is linked to our sense of balance and well-being (Lynch, 1960, p. 4).

It is not possible to address every medical and behavioral issue; each individual population and context is unique. However, we can assemble a list of characteristic behaviors of people who may gain some healing benefit from an outdoor environment designed to address their specific needs. For many cognitive impairments, such as mental illness, the outward signs of the suffering individual are rarely visible. Diseases of the mind include depression and schizophrenia, which are often misdiagnosed and misunderstood. The symptoms are not as apparent because they are rarely outwardly physical—for example, a young adult who suffers from schizophrenia may have an altered perception of his or her surroundings and suffer from fears that cannot be explained. The environment, therefore, if calming and secure, may ameliorate these feelings of anxiety (AMI of Wisconsin, 1996). However, with young people the social and physical environment should encourage continued integration and participation in some form of gainful work or occupation.

Cognitive disorders are distinct from physical disabilities. From a holistic approach to medicine, it may be argued that it is impossible to separate the two; however, for the purposes of clarity, it is necessary (APA, DSM-IV, 1994). Usually these disorders are associated with some illness or disability and have distinguishing behavioral characteristics. The two most common cognitive disorders are *delirium* and *dementia*.

Delirium is defined as a "disturbance of consciousness" that may manifest itself in a diminished clarity of awareness and attentiveness to the environment. Other characteristic features include memory impairment, disorientation, and perceptual disturbance not related to a preexisting or evolving dementia. Most often the disturbance is short-lived and comes and goes during the course of its progression (APA, DSM-IV, 1994). A therapeutic response to delirium may be to provide a clearly defined spatial order to the physical environment.

Dementia, historically linked with senility and old age, is also often misunderstood. "The essential feature of dementia is the development of multiple cognitive deficits that include memory impairment and at least one of the following cognitive disturbances: aphasia, apraxia, agnosia or a disturbance in executive functioning" (APA, DSM-IV, 1994, p. 134). *Aphasia* is characterized by diminished ability to link a name with a person or object. *Apraxia* is characterized as a diminished ability to perform basic motor activities despite the physical ability and comprehension of the task. *Agnosia* is the inability to recognize objects although the sensory functions are completely intact (APA, DSM-IV, 1994). For example, you may see clearly a chair and not be able to recall the name and, although completely aware of what a chair is used for, may not be able to complete the action of seating yourself without assistance. Impaired spatial orientation, difficulty in accurately judging physical abilities, and a shuffling walking pattern increases the possibility of falls.

Although the most common cause of dementia is Alzheimer's disease, there are multiple other causes including HIV, head trauma, Parkinson's disease, Huntington's disease, Pick's disease, and Creutzfeldt-Jakob's disease. Adapted from the *Diagnostic and Statistical Manual of Mental Disorders IV,* 1994, the following descriptions give a brief overview of each type of dementia.

Dementia associated with HIV infection is manifested by "forgetfulness, slowness, poor concentration, and difficulties with problem solving." Social behaviors are often affected, leading to apathy and social withdrawal. Delirium, delusions, and hallucinations may accompany the condition as well.

Dementia associated with head trauma depends on the type and extent of the brain injury. Typically, head trauma is associated with young males and risk-taking behaviors (motorcycle accidents) resulting in post-traumatic amnesia, which is often followed by memory impairment. Typical behaviors and cognitive impairments include attention problems, aphasia, anxiety, depression, apathy, increased aggression, or other personality changes although often sensory and motor skills are intact.

Parkinson's disease is usually associated with older people and characteristic features include slowing of cognition and motor abilities and impairment in memory recall and executive functions. Often the loss of control and diminishing cognition is accompanied by depression.

Huntington's disease affects people in their late thirties and forties, although the age range of cases is from 4 to 85. Characteristic of other dementias, Huntington's disease is a "progressive degenerative disease of cognition, emotion and movement" (APA, DSM-IV, 1994, p. 149). Pick's disease affects people age 50 to 60 years old and is characterized by personality changes. Social skills deteriorate, and often it is difficult to distinguish from Alzheimer's disease. Creutzfeldt-Jakob's disease is a slow virus transmission that affects the central nervous system and, like Huntington's disease and Pick's disease, is associated with middle-age ranges (40 to 60). In the later stages, behavioral characteristics include problems with concentration, incoordination, altered vision, and abnormal gait. The progression is rapid, but in rare instances it is seen over a period of years.

With an understanding of some characteristic behaviors, it is then necessary to begin to investigate possible sites for the garden or outdoor area most appropriate for specified users and develop a program of use.

Choosing Sites and Conducting Inventory

When does the actual site-specific design process begin? Often a garden design project begins with the realization of the potential for offering residents or patients a pleasant outdoor area. An individual or group of key advisors expresses an interest or makes a commitment to proceeding with this type of project. They have the land or an existing courtyard and an image of a place where residents or patients will walk, visit, enjoy the sunshine and fresh air, or do a little planting. Determining locations of outdoor spaces, proximity to other activities, relationship to indoor space, sun exposure, and the role of management have a direct impact on the frequency of and overall preference for use (Bite and Lovering, 1984, 1985; Carstens, 1985, 1990; Regnier, 1985).The elderly, for example, have a higher sensitivity to temperature, light, and noise. This hightened sensitivity may also exist for younger people as a result of illness and medications.

There may be very definite plans for a specific site, various possible locations from which to choose or a series of courtyards and open areas to design as part of the site project. Each individual site has a unique set of microclimate issues, landscape features, vegetation, and solar orientation that will determine potential use and design. When your users are clearly defined, the next step is to evaluate the site conditions to determine if they support the users' needs.

Documenting Existing Site Conditions

Documenting the existing physical conditions is basically mapping out what already exists on the site. Things to note are buildings, doors, windows, patios, trees, hills—any and all elements that make up the present site. It is helpful to note movable items like chairs, tables, umbrellas, and planters. Gather as much information as possible. You can evaluate the different factors that make up the site later; at this point just note everything. There may be site features that will remain as they exist or areas not directly related to your project site; if they are recorded now, it will save time later. These issues will be determined at a later phase of the design process. A detailed analysis of the site will be necessary before construction documents are prepared and final design decisions made. This analysis will usually include architectural layout and features, existing vegetation, utility lines, prevailing winds, solar orientation, existing permanent features and those to be removed, topography, drainage and grading flows, indigenous plant species, soil types and conditions, and any other pertinent site information (Mayhew, 1997).

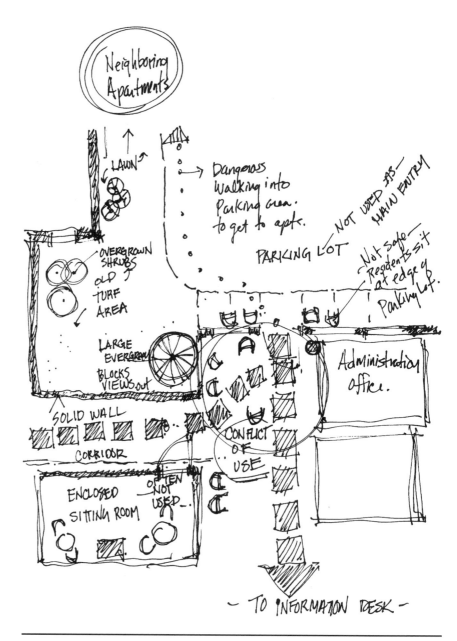

Patterns of use.

Formulate Therapeutic Goals

When working with impaired or ill populations, it is often difficult or impossible to obtain direct information through use of the formal research methods. A direct working relationship between the caregivers and designer will reveal specific behaviors that may be affected by the design of the physical environment. Consider the social environment as well as the physical surroundings in formulating your therapeutic goals. The following therapeutic goals are given as examples when considering people who may be living in an extended-care facility for rehabilitation purposes or residential care settings. As each design and research project is unique, the following goals are given as suggestions for developing more specific therapeutic goals and design objectives as each project requires.

When formulating therapeutic goals, we take a step back to review the initial mandate: to respond to individuals' needs and improve the healing connection between people and the natural world. The overall purpose of therapeutic goals for residents or patients is to assist people in achieving or maintaining the highest level of functioning (physical and psychosocial) and general well-being (Carstens, 1995; Cohen and Weisman, 1991).

We may take for granted our ability to do everyday things such as feeding the birds, watering plants, sitting in the sun, listening to music, preparing a meal, working on projects, taking a stroll in the sun, or simply looking out of a window. We see them as ordinary events; however, for many people, working toward and accomplishing these activities may be precisely what can make the day worthwhile. Our goal is to prepare the groundwork for the design of places to facilitate these ordinary, yet profound activities of everyday life.

The following are suggestions for beginning the exploration of specific therapeutic goals for residents/patients, staff, and family and visitors:

Residents/Patients' Therapeutic Goals

- *Support abilities, and compensate for losses* Through program development and interviews with residents, patients, staff, or therapists, determine resident or patient capabilities in completing tasks involved in garden-related or outdoor activities. Specific goals should accommodate and support both the social and physical abilities.
- *Instill a sense of belonging and usefulness* The designed environment and program should be structured to involve residents or patients in the care and upkeep of their home environment as part of their everyday routine.
- *Provide opportunities to continue work, trades, or hobbies* Consider residents' past experiences and occupations. Provide facilities, and tailor individual programs to encourage continuing with established social roles or developing interests in new skills or hobbies.
- *Establish connections to the familiar* Integrate familiar elements into the design in order to create a social environment that en-

courages interaction with other people and with the cultural context of surroundings.

- *Establish a sense of personal pride or ownership*   People need to identify personally with their surroundings. This can be achieved by providing areas where residents or patients can bring things from home and display familiar possessions and over which they can exert some control.

- *Maintain a sense of security in physical surroundings*   Provide easily recognized landmarks, predictable paths, and "safety zones" where residents can feel secure. Provide direct access, both visually and physically, to the indoors. Clearly mark the entrances from indoors and outdoors.

- *Heighten awareness of nature, seasons, places, and time*   Provide residents physical and visual access to the outdoors. This will allow them to connect with their immediate surroundings and the world at large. Use plantings with cultural, geographic, or seasonal interest.

- *Create places for physical exercise*   Residents or patients need a place to walk or get outdoors. The garden area should feel secure but not restrictive, and it should encourage exercise and movement as people are able.

- *Maximize a sense of independence and freedom*   Create an open environment, both socially and physically, that encourages residents to maintain their role as independent adults, capable of making their own decisions. Keep doors unlocked, and minimize the use of monitored or alarmed doorways and exits to secured outdoor areas.

Staff Therapeutic Goals

In order to provide a quality outdoor environment for residents, it is critical that staff needs are addressed. The support and involvement of the primary caregivers, who work directly with the residents, are essential for a successful program or design. An outdoor environment that addresses only the needs of residents follows a more clinical approach to design where the physical layout responds only to the residents' abilities. An integrated social atmosphere that considers the needs of residents, staff, and family is more complete.

- *Create a pleasant work environment*   The staff need to be comfortable with their surroundings to be able to integrate new ideas and programs that best meet the needs of residents. Staff input and participation will help create an atmosphere of working together.

- *Provide desired amount of space for activities* In order to best facilitate resident programs, the staff need adequate space. Sufficient available space can also determine the success of activity programs.
- *Allow for complete surveillance of area* The staff need the ability to observe residents both indoors and outdoors from several vantage points, while doing normal work-related tasks indoors.
- *Maintain flexibility to adapt environment* Layout and furnishings should facilitate staff alteration to meet residents' needs. Design and programming should be flexible and allow for adaptation by staff.
- *Provide places for resident/patient respite* Staff need places away from the main activity area to go with restless residents, to calm people, and to prevent disruption of other people or the overall atmosphere.
- *Designate places for staff breaks and respite* The staff need places away from the mainstream of activities to regain composure, to take a moment to readjust to stressful situations.
- *Provide ability to use space around the clock* Residents may be on an irregular sleep schedule, and so secure areas for walking and getting outdoors should be provided that can be used around the clock.
- *Establish direct access to outdoor areas* The staff need a designated and accessible entry and pathway that can accommodate the wandering and pacing that can occur with some ambulatory residents.

Families' and Visitors' Therapeutic Goals

Finally, the design must address the unique needs and concerns of family members and visitors. Time spent at the facility by family and visitors varies from daily visits to holiday or yearly visits. As with the frequency of use, the concerns and needs of family members vary. A well-designed outdoor living area can provide a unique opportunity for respite for people to visit, walk, or view from indoors.

- *Provide assurance that residents have quality care* Family members seek a place that will provide quality care and dignity for their loved one.
- *Provide a familiar homelike living environment* Family must feel comfortable with both the social and physical atmosphere of the home setting.
- *Offer social opportunities for residents/patients* Family members want to know that each resident may continue as normal a life as possible in comfortable surroundings.

- *Create a sense of privacy and comfort for visiting*   Family members need places to go when visiting the resident that will allow them to express emotions or discuss family matters away from other activities.
- *Encourage involvement with resident care program*   Some families may appreciate the opportunity to contribute to the specific programming and care of their family member. This may help new residents adjust to their new home.

Inviting Multidisciplinary Cooperation

Translating therapeutic goals into design objectives requires a multidisciplinary understanding of the common vision of the garden. The process of moving from theoretical concepts to objective physical qualities of landscape requires a clear common communication of images, meanings, and associations between design professionals and nondesign professionals. The interpretation of the nondesigner's perceived images, meanings, and emotional responses and aesthetic judgments needs to be considered as well as the designer's attention to function and appropriate fit in spatial terms and circulation (Uzzel and Lewand, 1990). This is in no uncertain terms the pivotal point of successful or unsuccessful design realization that responds to user needs. Terminology that overlaps disciplines can also be an area of potential misunderstanding. For example, the term *program* is understood by staff as an order of activities for residents, while to the architect, a *program* is the order of physical elements and spatial requirements to support and accommodate these social functions. The design response to a therapeutic goal begins to give spatial dimensions and to suggest physical features.

The input of staff will be most helpful at this stage of design development—for example, it may be desirable to have an area for five to seven people to gather in one part of the garden, while one individual can still feel free to stroll out along a pathway without intruding or being intruded upon. The therapist may have a clear idea of the program and benefits, however not be able to visualize the spatial requirements and relationships between garden functions.

Will the area be a paved surface or lawn? Will there be shelter from the sun? Does the path pass through or around the place where people gather? These questions begin to require more than theoretical solutions that a design professional will assist in generating. One useful method is actually working together (designer and associated staff), measuring the area used by a group similar to the planned event and using that as a reference for creating a spatial architectural program for design. Using this process, the natural progression leads the group to begin to define physical features of landscapes and gardens. The next part of the process involves application of therapeutic goals into the language of design.

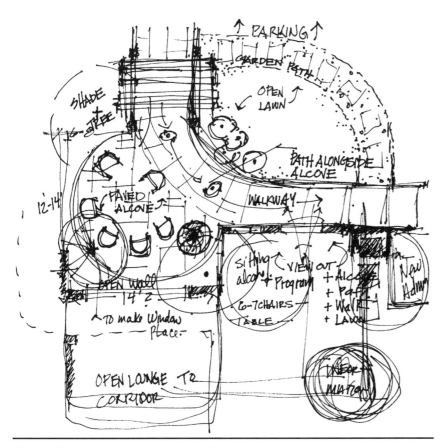

On-site layout gives correct proportions.

Applying Patterns to Design

The design objectives represent a cross-disciplinary evaluation of litera-ture and research focused on designed environments for special-needs populations, including the elderly, physically or cognitively impaired, and ill. Characteristic behaviors and physiological symptoms cover the range from mild to severe impairment.

The objectives are categorized in terms of *individual needs* (e.g., safety and security or privacy), the *environment* (e.g., comfortable micro-climate or residential character), and the *interaction* between individuals and the environment (i.e., spatial orientation or sensory awareness).

Each directive has two subobjectives that address separate issues listed in the general heading (e.g., "safety and security" involves both staff surveillance as well as physical enclosure to assure the safety of resi-dents). These objectives are used in subsequent stages of the process as a basis for defining design theory and developing design patterns. Matrix diagrams show the relationship between the therapeutic goals and design objectives. These directives were compiled and adapted from a number of research and design sources, including Anderson,

1990; Carey, 1986; Carpman et al., 1986; Carstens, 1985; Cohen and Weisman, 1991; Cooper Marcus and Barnes, 1995; Cooper Marcus and Francis, 1990; Hagedorn, 1990; Healy, 1997; Lewis, 1995; Regnier, 1994; Stoneham and Thoday, 1996.

DESIGN OBJECTIVES

I. Person: Individual's Needs
  1. Provide safety and security for residents/patients
     a. Full staff surveillance from indoors
     b. Enclosed grounds
  2. Promote independence
     a. Freedom to go outdoors
     b. Accessible pathways
  3. Heighten sensory awareness
     a. Selection of plant material
     b. Strategic location of highly sensory plantings
  4. Ensure personal privacy
     a. Plantings as buffers from direct intrusion
     b. Semiprivate sitting alcoves
  5. Encourage ownership
     a. Ability to adapt environment
     b. Individual and community gardens
II. Place: Physical Environment
  1. Integrate indoor and outdoor areas
     a. Windows overlooking outdoor area
     b. Comfortable transition at entrances
  2. Create comfortable microclimate
     a. Physical protection from elements
     b. Plantings to mitigate extremes in temperature
  3. Create familiar character
     a. Residential construction materials
     b. Context and character fit to function
III. Interaction: Behavior
  1. Encourage social and environmental interaction
     a. Places for people to gather
     b. Places for people to encounter nature
  2. Support a range of abilities
     a. Access for active use
     b. Observation and passive activities
  3. Maximize spatial orientation
     a. Simple layout
     b. Strategic use of landmarks
  4. Provide interesting walking paths
     a. Experience of passage
     b. Exercise and movement
  5. Provide seating choices
     a. Places for visiting
     b. Quiet places
  6. Provide places for work and recreation
     a. Gardening workbench
     b. Outdoor sports

Therapeutic Goals for Residents or Patients

Support abilities and compensate for losses
Establish connections to the familiar
Instill a sense of belonging and usefulness
Establish a sense of pride or ownership in surroundings
Provide opportunities to continue with work or hobbies
Maintain sense of security in physical surroundings
Heighten awareness of nature, seasons, places and time
Create places for physical exercise
Maximize a sense of independence and freedom

Design Matrix

Goals →	Support abilities	Connections	Sense of belonging	Ownership	Security	Work/ hobbies	Awareness	Exercise	Independence
Person: individual's needs									
Safety and security	✔		✔		✔				
Promote independence	✔		✔	✔	✔	✔		✔	✔
Sensory awareness		✔					✔	✔	
Personal privacy			✔		✔				✔
Ownership		✔		✔		✔			
Place: physical environment									
Integrate indoors		✔			✔		✔		
Microclimate	✔				✔	✔			✔
Walking paths	✔						✔	✔	✔
Familiar character		✔	✔		✔		✔		
Interaction: behavior									
Interaction	✔			✔			✔		
Range of abilities	✔	✔	✔			✔		✔	✔
Spatial orientation	✔				✔		✔	✔	✔
Seating choices				✔	✔			✔	✔
Familiar tasks	✔	✔	✔	✔		✔			✔

Therapeutic Goals for
Staff

Create a pleasant work environment

Provide desired amount of space for activities

Allow for complete surveillance of area

Maintain flexibility to adapt environment to changing needs

Provide places for resident respite from stress

Create places for staff breaks and respite

Provide ability to use space around the clock

Establish pathway system for agitated residents

Implement innovative therapeutic programming

Design Matrix

Goals →	Pleasant work	Activity space	Surveillance	Flexibility	Patient respite	Staff respite	Around the clock	Path system	Programming
Person: individual's needs									
Safety and security	✔		✔				✔	✔	
Promote independence		✔		✔	✔		✔	✔	✔
Sensory awareness					✔	✔			✔
Personal privacy	✔				✔	✔			
Ownership		✔		✔					✔
Place: physical environment									
Integrate indoors			✔		✔	✔	✔		✔
Microclimate	✔	✔		✔	✔	✔	✔		✔
Walking paths	✔				✔			✔	
Familiar character	✔				✔				✔
Interaction: behavior									
Interaction	✔	✔	✔	✔	✔	✔		✔	
Range of abilities		✔	✔	✔				✔	✔
Spatial orientation			✔				✔	✔	
Seating choices	✔			✔		✔			
Familiar tasks					✔				✔

Therapeutic Goals for Families and Visitors

Provide assurance that residents have quality care

Provide a familiar homelike living environment

Opportunities for residents to continue normal social roles

Create a sense of privacy and comfortable visiting places

Encourage involvement with resident care program

Design Matrix

Goals →	Quality assurance	Home environment	Social roles	Visiting places	Involvement
Person: individual's needs					
Safety and security	✔			✔	
Promote independence	✔		✔		
Sensory awareness	✔				
Personal privacy				✔	✔
Ownership		✔			✔
Place: physical environment					
Integrate indoors		✔		✔	
Microclimate	✔			✔	
Walking paths	✔				
Familiar character		✔	✔	✔	✔
Interaction: behavior					
Interaction	✔		✔	✔	
Range of abilities	✔		✔		✔
Spatial orientation	✔	✔			
Seating choices		✔		✔	
Familiar tasks			✔		✔

CHAPTER 2

Design

Translate into Design Patterns

To establish the foundation of developing a design language made up of patterns, we first need to define the term *pattern*. Patterns are occurrences that happen over and over in the built environment. Patterns are often archetypal, "so deeply rooted in the nature of things that it seems likely that they will be a part of human nature in five hundred years as they are today." Patterns are the elements of the language of design. Patterns are like the individual words or phrases that are combined when creating prose or poetry. Patterns are generated from keen observation of human social behavior and the environments we build to support these activities. Patterns are derived from in-depth study of the characteristic behaviors and needs of particular groups of people in particular settings. Patterns are those elements of places that give meaning and form to our images. In a later part of this section we will discuss methods of developing a new pattern language, "taking as a point of departure" the language of patterns printed in *A Pattern Language* (Alexander et al., 1977, p. xvii).

A sequence of patterns was chosen from the summary of the language found in *The Timeless Way of Building* and *A Pattern Language*. The two are the first and second in a series of three books describing a process of designing and building environments that is rooted in universal relationships between people and their surroundings. Of the 253 patterns, 25 were selected based on the environmental and behavioral characteristics that best addressed the therapeutic goals formulated in Chap. 1, although there are many more applicable to the design of landscapes. A brief description of each is taken from the in-depth explanations given for each pattern. (*Note on reading the pattern:* The asterisks ** represent the degree of faith the authors have in the reliability of the pattern hypothesis.)

Pattern 69
Public Outdoor Room**

"In every neighborhood and work community, make a piece of the common land into an outdoor room—a partially enclosed place, with some roof, columns, without walls, perhaps with a trellis; place it beside an important path and within view of many homes and workshops."

Alexander et al., 1977, p. 351

A place along the path.

DESIGN OBJECTIVES

Person: Individual's Needs
Provide for safety and security.
Promote independence.
Allow for privacy.

Place: Physical Environment
Integrate indoor and outdoor areas.
Create comfortable microclimate.

Interaction: Behavior
Create interactive environment.
Consider a range of abilities.

Pattern 79
Your Own Home**

"Give every household its own home, with space enough for a garden. Indeed, where it is possible to construct forms of ownership which give people control over their houses and gardens,...choose these forms above all others. In all cases give people legal power, and the physical opportunity to modify and repair their own places...."

Alexander et al., 1977, p. 395

Marlene admires her garden.

DESIGN OBJECTIVES

Person: Individual's Needs
Provide for safety and security.
Promote independence.
Encourage ownership.

Place: Physical Environment
Create comfortable microclimate.

Interaction: Behavior
Create interactive environment.
Consider a range of abilities.
Allow for work and recreation.

Pattern 106
Positive Outdoor Space**

"Make all the outdoor spaces which surround and lie between your buildings positive. Give each one some degree of enclosure; surround each space with wings of buildings, trees, hedges, fences, arcades, and trellised walks, until it becomes an entity with a positive quality and does not spill out indefinitely around corners."   *Alexander et al., 1977, p. 522*

A sense of enclosure.

DESIGN OBJECTIVES

Person: Individual's Needs
Provide for safety and security.
Allow for heightened sensory awareness.

Place: Physical Environment
Create comfortable microclimate.
Provide interesting walking paths.

Interaction: Behavior
Maximize spatial orientation.
Encourage social and environmental interaction.

Pattern 114
Hierarchy of Open Space

"Whatever space you are shaping—whether it is a garden, terrace, street, park, public outdoor room, or courtyard—make sure of two things. First, make at least one smaller space, which looks into it and forms a natural back for it. Second, place it, and its openings, so that it looks into at least one larger space. When you have done this, every outdoor space will have a natural "back," and every person who takes up the natural position, with his back to this "back," will be looking out toward some larger distant view."   *Alexander et al., 1977, p. 559*

A place to sit and think.

DESIGN OBJECTIVES

Person: Individual's Needs
Provide for safety and security.
Allow for privacy.

Interaction: Behavior
Maximize spatial orientation.
Provide a variety of seating choices.

Pattern 115
Courtyards Which Live**

"Place every courtyard in such a way that there is view out of it to some larger open space; place it so that at least two or three doors open from the building into it and so that the natural paths which connect these doors open from the building into it and so that the natural paths which connect these doors pass across the courtyard. And, at one edge, beside a door, make a roofed veranda or a porch, which is continuous with both the inside and the courtyard...."

Alexander et al., 1977, p. 564

A place to say hello.

DESIGN OBJECTIVES

Person: Individual's Needs
Encourage personalization.

Place: Physical Environment
Create residential character.
Provide interesting walking paths.

Interaction: Behavior
Create interactive environment.
Consider a range of abilities.

Pattern 119
Arcades**

"Wherever paths run along the edge of buildings, build arcades, and use the arcades, above all, to connect up the buildings to one another, so that a person can walk from place to place under the cover of the arcades."

Alexander et al., 1977, p. 583

Protected from the rain.

DESIGN OBJECTIVES

Place: Physical Environment
Integrate indoor and outdoor space.
Provide interesting walking paths.

Interaction: Behavior
Create interactive environment.

Pattern 120
Paths and Goals*

"To lay out the paths, first place goals at natural points of interest. Then connect the goals to one another to form the paths. The paths may be straight, or gently curving between the goals; their paving should swell around the goal. The goals should never be more than a few hundred feet apart."

Alexander et al., 1977, p. 587

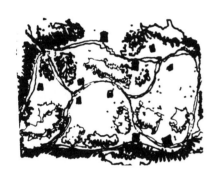

Events along the way.

DESIGN OBJECTIVES

Person: Individual's Needs
Provide for safety and security.
Promote independence.

Place: Physical Environment
Provide interesting walking paths.

Interaction: Behavior
Create interactive environment.
Consider a range of abilities.
Maximize spatial orientation.

Pattern 121
Path Shape*

"Make a bulge in the middle of a public path, and make the ends narrower, so that the path forms an enclosure which is a place to stay, not just a place to pass through."

Alexander et al., 1977, p. 591

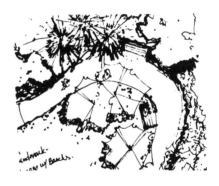

A place to stop and rest.

DESIGN OBJECTIVES

Person: Individual's Needs
Promote independence.
Allow for privacy.

Place: Physical Environment
Provide interesting walking paths.

Interaction: Behavior
Create interactive environment.
Maximize spatial orientation.
Provide a variety of seating choices.

Pattern 124
Activity Pockets**

"Surround public gathering places with pockets of activity—small, partly enclosed areas at the edges, which jut forward into the open space between the paths, and contain activities which make it natural for people to pause and get involved."   *Alexander et al., 1977, p. 607*

An invitation to come inside.

DESIGN OBJECTIVES

Person: Individual's Needs
Promote independence.

Place: Physical Environment
Provide interesting walking paths.

Interaction: Behavior
Create interactive environment.
Provide a variety of seating choices.

Pattern 126
Something Roughly in the Middle

"Between the natural paths which cross a public square or courtyard or a piece of common land, choose something to stand roughly in the middle: a fountain, a tree, a statue, a clock-tower with seats, a windmill, a bandstand. Make it something which gives a strong and steady pulse to the square, drawing people in toward the center. Leave it exactly where it falls between the paths; resist the impulse to put it exactly in the middle."   *Alexander et al., 1977, p. 601*

The courtyard tree.

DESIGN OBJECTIVES

Place: Physical Environment
Provide interesting walking paths.

Interaction: Behavior
Create interactive environment.
Maximize spatial orientation.

Pattern 127
Intimacy Gradient

"Lay out the spaces of a building so that they create a sequence which begins with the entrance and the most public parts of the building, then leads into the slightly more private areas, and finally to the most private domains."

Alexander et al., 1977, p. 613

Sequence of places.

DESIGN OBJECTIVES

Person: Individual's Needs
Allow for privacy.

Interaction: Behavior
Create interactive environment.
Consider a range of abilities.
Provide a variety of seating choices.

Pattern 129
Common Areas at the Heart**

"Create a single common area for every social group. Locate it at the center of gravity of all the spaces the group occupies, and in such a way that the paths which go in and out of the building lie tangent to it."

Alexander et al., 1977, p. 621

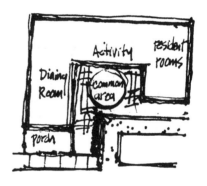

A centrally located patio.

DESIGN OBJECTIVES

Person: Individual's Needs
Provide for safety and security.
Promote independence.

Place: Physical Environment
Create residential character.
Provide interesting walking paths.

Interaction: Behavior
Create interactive environment.
Maximize spatial orientation.

Pattern 142
Sequence of Sitting Spaces*

"Put in a sequence of sitting spaces throughout the building, varying according to their degree of enclosure. Enclose the most formal ones entirely, in rooms by themselves; put the least formal ones in corners of the rooms, without any kind of screen around them; and place the intermediate ones with a partial enclosure round them to keep them connected to some larger space, but also partly separate."

Alexander et al., 1977, p. 674

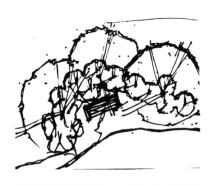

A pathway alcove.

DESIGN OBJECTIVES

Person: Individual's Needs
Allow for privacy.

Place: Physical Environment
Create residential character.
Provide interesting walking paths.

Interaction: Behavior
Create interactive environment.
Maximize spatial orientation.
Provide a variety of seating choices.

Pattern 156
Settled Work*

"Give each person, especially as he grows old, the chance to set up a workplace of his own, within or very near his home. Make it a place that can grow slowly, perhaps in the beginning sustaining a weekend hobby and gradually becoming a complete, productive and comfortable workshop."   *Alexander et al., 1977, p. 735*

Watering the flowers.

DESIGN OBJECTIVES

Person: Individual's Needs
Promote independence.
Allow for heightened sensory awareness.
Encourage personalization.

Place: Physical Environment
Create residential character.

Interaction: Behavior
Create interactive environment.
Consider a range of abilities.
Continue familiar tasks.

Pattern 161
Sunny Place**

"Inside a south-facing court, or garden, or yard, find the spot between the building and outdoors which gets the best sun. Develop this spot as a special sunny place—make it the important outdoor room, a place to work in the sun, or a place for a swing and some special plants, a place to sunbathe. Be very careful indeed to place the sunny place in a position where it is sheltered from the wind. A steady wind will prevent you from using the most beautiful place." *Alexander et al., 1977, p. 759*

Enjoying the sunshine.

DESIGN OBJECTIVES

Person: Individual's Needs
Promote independence.
Allow for heightened sensory awareness.

Place: Physical Environment
Create residential character.

Interaction: Behavior
Create interactive environment.
Consider a range of abilities.
Continue familiar tasks.

Pattern 171
Tree Places**

"If you are planting trees, plant them according to their nature, to form enclosures, avenues, squares, groves, and single spreading trees toward the middle of open spaces. And shape the nearby buildings in response to trees, so that the tree themselves, and the trees and buildings together, form places which people can use." *Alexander et al., 1977, p. 800*

Shady walking.

DESIGN OBJECTIVES

Person: Individual's Needs
Allow for heightened sensory awareness.

Interaction: Behavior
Create interactive environment.
Maximize spatial orientation.

Pattern 173
Garden Wall*

"Form some kind of enclosure to protect the interior of a quiet garden from the sights and sounds of passing traffic. If it is a large garden or a park, the enclosure can be soft, can include bushes, trees, slopes, and so on. The smaller the garden, however, the harder and more definite the enclosure must become. In a very small garden, form the enclosure with buildings or walls; even hedges and fences will not be enough to keep out sound."

Alexander et al., 1977, p. 807

A sense of arrival.

DESIGN OBJECTIVES

Person: Individual's Needs
Provide for safety and security.
Allow for privacy.

Place: Physical Environment
Create comfortable microclimate.
Create residential character.

Interaction: Behavior
Create interactive environment.
Provide a variety of seating choices.

Pattern 176
Garden Seat

"Make a quiet place in the garden—a private enclosure with a comfortable seat, thick planting, sun. Pick the place for the seat very carefully; pick the place that will give you the most intense kind of solitude."

Alexander et al., 1977, p. 817

A quiet resting place.

DESIGN OBJECTIVES

Person: Individual's Needs
Allow for heightened sensory awareness.
Allow for privacy.

Place: Physical Environment
Create comfortable microclimate.
Create residential character.

Interaction: Behavior
Create interactive environment.
Maximize spatial orientation.
Provide a variety of seating choices.

Pattern 177
Vegetable Garden*

"Set aside one piece of land either in the private garden or on common land as a vegetable garden. About one-tenth of an acre is needed for each family of four. Make sure the vegetable garden is in a sunny place and central to all the households it serves. Fence it in and build a small storage shed for gardening tools beside it."

Alexander et al., 1977, p. 820

Harvesting the corn.

DESIGN OBJECTIVES

Person: Individual's Needs
Promote independence.
Allow for heightened sensory awareness.
Encourage personalization.

Place: Physical Environment
Create residential character.

Interaction: Behavior
Create interactive environment.
Consider a range of abilities.
Continue familiar tasks.

Pattern 179
Alcoves**

"Make small places at the edge of any common room, usually no more than 6 feet wide and 3 to 6 feet deep and possibly much smaller. These alcoves should be large enough for two people to sit, chat, or play and sometimes large enough to contain a desk or a table."

Alexander et al., 1977, p. 832

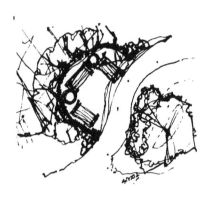

A place to visit.

DESIGN OBJECTIVES

Person: Individual's Needs
Promote independence.
Allow for privacy.

Place: Physical Environment
Create residential character.
Create interesting paths.

Interaction: Behavior
Consider a range of abilities.
Maximize spatial orientation.
Provide a variety of seating choices.

Pattern 185
Sitting Circles*

"Place each sitting space in a position which is protected, not cut by paths or movement, roughly circular, made so that the room itself helps to suggest the circle—not too strongly— with paths and activities around it, so that people naturally gravitate towards the chairs when they get in the mood to sit. Place the chairs and cushions loosely in the circle, and have a few too many."   *Alexander et al., 1977, p. 859*

Group discussions.

DESIGN OBJECTIVES

Person: Individual's Needs
Allow for privacy.
Encourage personalization.

Place: Physical Environment
Integrate indoor and outdoor spaces.
Create comfortable microclimate.
Create residential character.

Interaction: Behavior
Create interactive environment.
Provide a variety of seating choices.

Pattern 201
Waist-High Shelf

"Build waist-high shelves around at least part of the main rooms where people live and work. Make them long, 9 to 15 inches deep, with shelves or cupboards underneath. Interrupt the shelf for seats, windows and doors."
Alexander et al., 1977, p. 922

A place to work.

DESIGN OBJECTIVES

Person: Individual's Needs
Promote independence.
Encourage personalization.

Place: Physical Environment
Create residential character.

Interaction: Behavior
Consider a range of abilities.
Maximize spatial orientation.
Continue familiar tasks.

Pattern 241
Seat Spots**

"Choosing good spots for outdoor seats is far more important than building fancy benches. Indeed, if the spot is right, the most simple kind of seat is perfect. In cool climates, choose them to face the sun, and to be protected from the wind; in hot climates, put them in shade and open to summer breezes. In both cases, place them to face activities."

Alexander et al., 1977, p. 1120

A sunny sitting place.

DESIGN OBJECTIVES

Person: Individual's Needs
Promote independence.
Allow for heightened sensory awareness.

Place: Physical Environment
Create interesting paths.

Interaction: Behavior
Consider a range of abilities.
Maximize spatial orientation.
Provide a variety of seating choices.

Pattern 242
Front Door Bench**

"Build a special bench outside the front door where people from inside can sit comfortably for hours on end and watch the world go by. Place the bench to define a half-private domain in front of the house. A low wall, planting, a tree, can help to create the same domain."

Alexander et al., 1977, p. 1123

A comfortable place.

DESIGN OBJECTIVES

Person: Individual's Needs
Promote independence.
Encourage ownership.

Place: Physical Environment
Integrate indoors and outdoors.
Create comfortable microclimate.
Create familiar character.

Interaction: Behavior
Consider a range of abilities.
Maximize spatial orientation.
Provide a variety of seating choices.

Pattern 245
Raise Flowers*

"Soften the edges of buildings, paths and outdoor areas with flowers. Raise the flower beds so that people can touch the flowers, bend to touch them, and sit by them. And build the flower beds with solid edges, so that people can sit on them, among the flowers too."

Alexander et al., 1977, p. 1134

Growing flowers.

DESIGN OBJECTIVES

Person: Individual's Needs
Allow for heightened sensory awareness.
Ensure personal privacy.

Place: Physical Environment
Create familiar character.

Interaction: Behavior
Create interactive environment

Developing a Pattern Language for Design

After the introduction to the use of patterns and some understanding of what is meant by a *design pattern,* we will embark on the process of creating a new set of design patterns. These patterns will be *generated from* the therapeutic goals in Chap. 1 and supported by the design objectives and selected patterns from *A Pattern Language.*

Translating the abstract into physical design terms requires the use of problem-solving or design methods that bridge the gap between the linear scientific path of thinking and the intuitive or artistic line of thought. For example, when working with information structured for people from scientific backgrounds (e.g., medical training, administration, or social science), it is important for designers to have the ability to encourage creative problem solving with people trained to focus on a scientific way of communicating and problem solving. "Creativity is basic problem-solving that relates to any field—putting together two existing ideas to form something new and beneficial." This quote from Dr. Betty Edwards, Ph.D., researcher and art professor, opens the discussion of translating therapeutic goals into a language of design patterns. The process of this translation requires us first to look at how the translation process occurs in the brain. The left hemisphere of the brain is dominated by verbal functions such as language and reasoning, while the right hemisphere controls the visual or imaging activity of the brain (Heim, 1985).

There is more going on in your brain than you might think. How we learn, see and remember are complex processes based as much on previous experience as current information that we receive from our senses. Even simple daily tasks, both physical and intellectual, are actually complicated maneuvers involving perception, comprehension and cognition. Your brain juggles and combines a variety of sensory information in order to make sense of the world around you (Brookhart et al., 1992).

Creativity research illustrates how using a linguistic device such as a list of relation words (e.g., *to, under, about, between,* and *opposite*) may help in problem solving, or action words (e.g., *modify, magnify, adapt, substitute,* and *reverse*) for inducing transformations in thought (Chen, 1985). An example of this is the choice of words used in the therapeutic goal: *support abilities and compensate for losses.* By using the word *support* as it relates to the *ability to walk,* we can formulate possible ways to assist people with walking by providing accessible and clearly defined paths.

Using the word *compensate* as it relates to an *impaired gait,* we can formulate ways to provide for necessary prosthetic supports (e.g., handrails for balance or benches for resting).

A handrail to compensate for impaired balance and clear walkway.

A bench to support walking and resting along the way.

The example shows how the problem-solving method assists in translating the descriptions of therapeutic goals into descriptions of design patterns into elements of the garden or landscape.

According to research conducted through the National Foundation for Brain Research, explorers in brain research are searching for a greater understanding of the function of the brain and how social and behavioral interactions are connected to the brain:

The study of thinking, learning and memory is based on the idea that thinking relies on the interpretation of symbols, which provide us with a kind of shorthand, both saving time and space and providing a logic and organization which our brains can handle. The ability to create and use symbols in order to understand, store and recall things about the world is the essential feature of intelligence. One of the most prominent intellectual activities that depends on symbols, as well as memory, is language (Brookhart et al., 1992).

In the study of language and creative writing, there are specific terms used to describe the varied patterns of language. The term *cadence* is used to describe the "rhythmic flow of language that provides the sense of continuity and wholeness in writing" and *recurrence* to describe "the meaningful repetition of words, images, phrases, sounds, objects or actions throughout a piece of writing to unify and empower it" (Rico, 1983, pp. 111, 135). The term *Metaphor* is used to describe the joining of words and images to give us the character or quality of an idea (Rico, 1983). In this we begin to see the transformation of words to images or patterns. The composition of the words in sentences creates rhythms, and in poetry, we have a rhythmic whole. "The poet carefully controls his rhythms by the way he places the poem on the page; not even punctuation is necessary to guide the reader" (Rico, 1983, p. 148).

The Road Not Taken

Two roads diverged in a yellow wood,
And sorry I could not travel both
And be one traveler, long I stood
And looked down one as far as I could
To where it bent in the undergrowth;

Then took the other, as just as fair
And having perhaps the better claim,
Because it was grassy and wanted wear;
Though as for that the passage there
Had worn them really about the same,

And both that morning equally lay
In leaves no step had trodden black.
Oh, I kept the first for another day!
Yet knowing how way leads on to way,
I doubted if I should ever come back.

I shall be telling this with a sigh
Somewhere ages and ages hence:
Two roads diverged in a wood, and I—
I took the one less traveled by,
And that has made all the difference.

—Robert Frost, 1916, p. 131

Just as the application of *cadence*, *recurrence*, and *metaphor* creates patterns in the written language as poetry, the thoughtful composition of and relationships between design patterns produce the rhythm of the social life of a place with the natural elements of landscapes, bringing the design full circle and giving it meaning and purpose (Conley, 1997). "We need an environment which is not simply well organized, but poetic and symbolic as well" (Lynch, 1960, p. 119). The pattern of words in *prose* communicates ideas, often in a pleasing flow of language; however, words composed in the form of *true poetry* create more vivid images with deeper meaning. "In a poem, the meaning [of a word] is far more dense [than in prose]. Each word carries several meanings; and the sentence as a whole carries an enormous density of interlocking meanings, which together illuminate the whole" (Alexander et al., 1977, p. xli). "A poem may be worked over once it is in being, but may not be worried into being. Its most precious quality will remain its having run itself and carried away the poet with it. Read it a hundred times; it will forever keep its freshness as a metal keeps its fragrance. It can never lose its sense of a meaning that once unfolded by surprise as it went" (Frost, 1916, p. viii).

The life of a place is derived from a mix of culture, the people, the landscape; these are the elements of the language of the people and places that give them meaning and life. Language, poetry, and music all follow a sequence of patterns or rhythm. When translated from their native tongue, poetry and music often lose the life that brings a lilt to the melody or true emotion to the words. "Poetry,…is what is lost in translation" (Robert Frost as quoted on the NPR Broadcast University of the Air, 1997). To communicate this life without losing it in the translation, we use words to form images, and use images to give character and meaning to the physical forms we create. We will create a set of design patterns generated for the composition of landscapes with healing qualities. In the preceding section, we explored some of the patterns in *A Pattern Language* (Alexander et al., 1977), and we applied them to the therapeutic outcomes that we desired. The following series of new and adapted patterns was generated from that exploration. Using the theories of language and design, we began the exploration of the components of the healing garden. The therapeutic goals are used as both a generating device and a checking device to verify the fit of the design to the therapeutic intent. The patterns are also presented as sketches to help give a sense of physical and spatial form. The sketches illustrate how the design patterns may.support the therapeutic goals when applied to the design of a landscape. Refer to the design objectives to further define the relationship between the patterns and therapeutic goals. In an effort to make the research information more accessible, the subpatterns serve as a quick reference. By providing the written descriptions as well as a visual image, it is hoped

Bringing the outdoors in (Daniel Sjordal).

that both visually oriented and verbally oriented readers can better understand the thought process.

As an example, we will use the therapeutic goal: *to allow for complete surveillance of the outdoor area.* We will consider the words *allow* and *surveillance* to begin formulating images and ideas of how to accomplish this goal in the design. We may assume that somehow it is necessary to create a visual connection between indoors and the garden or surrounding landscape where patients or residents will spend time.

This can be accomplished by providing windows overlooking the outdoor area that are placed where staff are able to survey the area while accomplishing routine scheduled activities. Doors with a solid or partial window panel and low-level lighting are other possible solutions. A pattern of creating an integrated relationship between the indoor and outdoors, with several subpatterns, was developed to give more defined character and form.

To introduce the outdoor world to the indoor life of a place, there must be a conscious effort to integrate life indoors with the garden and surrounding landscape.

Subpatterns: Indoors and Outdoors

1. *Window place.*   Outdoor spaces should reflect life indoors. Indoor seating alcoves with low window sills may look out onto small

Window place.

Natural sunlight.

garden scenes or larger views. Resident rooms should be buffered from direct outdoor activity by an appropriate distance or plantings.

2. *Natural sunlight.*   Directly adjacent to the secured outdoor area should be places where natural sunlight can enter the indoors as well as provide views outside. Window treatments should be provided where needed to screen views or glare.

3. *Garden viewing places.*   Staff need some strategic vantage points from indoors to be able to observe residents using the outdoor area (during the normal routine of the day).

Garden viewing places.

Nighttime lighting.

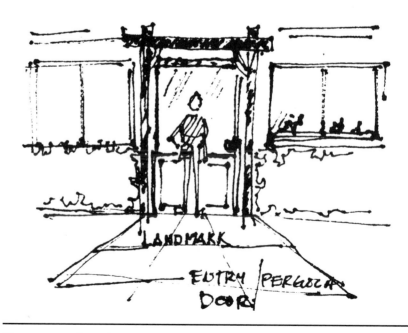

Doorways and entries.

4. *Doorways and entries.*   Doors and gateways to secured outdoor areas should be open to residents with full or partial glass panels for maximum visibility to outdoors. Entryways leading to the outdoor area should be easily recognized and accessible to residents. Staff may need visual or auditory cues when residents exit to the outdoors.

5. *Nighttime lighting.*   Lighting the outdoor areas extends the indoor living and activity areas. Low-level lighting will allow for evening use of outdoor seating areas and pathways. The use of lighting will bring the garden to life at twilight and throughout the evening hours. Pathway lighting can make safe walking possible in the evening hours.

Checking the Pattern for Reliability

Now, using the words *allow* and *surveillance* as key transformation cues, we can begin to check the pattern for its reliability in providing complete staff visibility. Providing windows into the outdoor area from key locations within the unit is one way to accomplish this goal. The specifics of window type and design and building edge will be further defined as the pattern begins to take form. Not every therapeutic goal will translate directly into a design pattern or series of patterns, nor will every design pattern necessarily solve all of the therapeutic goals. However, the dual system of thinking helps to check and verify that the design does in fact respond to the needs of the users and the original intent.

It may seem that the elements and patterns are quite ordinary. This is true. We often reach for those unusual and profound solutions while

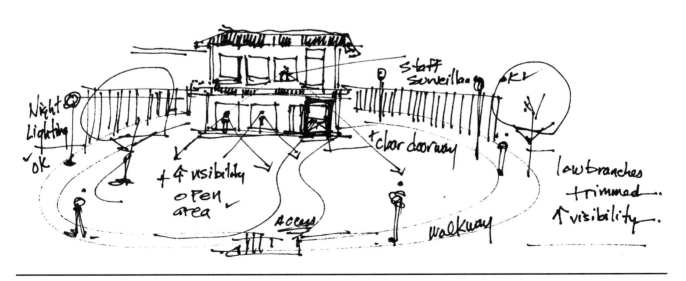

Checking visibility.

overlooking more solid solutions. We rarely look for them and find it hard to locate them because they are so ordinary; however, "it is because they are so ordinary, indeed that they strike to the core" (Alexander et al., 1979, p. 219). The healing process for people suffering from any type of illness will be enhanced by a place that is comfortable and familiar. Following this path of thought, a larger system of patterns was established including indoors and outdoors, paths and landmarks, garden places, enclosure, views, plantings, furnishings, and environmental cues (Zeisel and Tyson 1997). Now we will look at the pattern *pathways and landmarks.* The manner in which people enter into the garden area and are invited to move throughout depends on the inclusion and careful layout of paths and landmarks. A simple system of walkways, patios, and resting areas can provide staff with a familiar and interesting place where they can walk with patients or where patients with greater functional ability may safely move about on their own.

Subpatterns: Pathways and Landmarks

1. *The walking path.*   Create a primary walkway that brings people from the main entrance around or through the central outdoor area, connecting important gathering areas and entrances. It should be wide enough for two or three people to walk and talk side by side.

2. *The strolling garden path.*   A slightly meandering path through a naturally landscaped setting can provide a place for quiet walks and retreat. Trellises or arbors with vines or climbing flowers, seating alcoves or single benches, can offer opportunities to stop and rest along the way.

3. *Just around the corner.*   Every path should have a series of landmarks along the way to invite movement through the garden.

The strolling garden path.

The walking path.

Just around the corner.

Familiar destinations.

Familiar garden features (birdbaths, bird feeders, benches) can be used as landmarks to encourage movement along the paths through the outdoor space. Pathway landmarks should be placed within natural sight lines at a comfortable walking distance from each other.

   4. *Familiar destinations.*   Important destinations should be easily recognized and identified from all places along the path to facilitate orientation and way finding. Secondary landmarks can be used as way-finding cues and to create interest along the path. When given choices, create known and recognized points to reach smaller goals on the way to the destination.

   The next set of patterns, *garden places*, describe distinctive areas within the garden. There are natural social activities and everyday events that give distinctive form and character to particular places in the garden. From these social events and happenings are borne the garden places that bring the landscape to life.

Subpatterns: Garden Places

   1. *Open spaces.*   People enjoy open spaces to play, to watch squirrels scampering, or robins hunting for worms. An open area (courtyard, lawn, or terrace) provides an opportunity for distant views and a sense of freedom from the confinement of being indoors. Create an open area with sky and sunshine and pathways connecting places where people are.

Open spaces.

Working garden.

Gardener's workbench.

2. *Working garden.*　Without the events and activities of ordinary life, the garden is not complete. Provide places for people to continue with familiar tasks in a comfortable setting. Hanging towels over the porch railing to dry, potting geraniums, watering plants, feeding the birds, sweeping the patio, and raking leaves are examples of ways to imbue the garden with real life. Provide some places within the garden for doing work.

3. *Gardener's workbench.*　Provide a small shed for garden tools, a waist-high potting table and shelves, trellises for training roses, benches and tables for laying out projects. Provide each person opportunities for accomplishing some task and succeeding.

Gathering places.

Porches and terraces.

4. *Gathering places.*   Provide places for group gatherings, harvest celebrations, and picnics. The place should be located near indoor social spaces and activity and at the place where paths naturally cross. There should be at least one common gathering place along the primary pathway that people pass by often. The place should be comfortable for viewing the garden, visiting, and informal friendly greetings.

5. *Porches and terraces.*   Porches or terraces adjacent to indoor activity areas should accommodate group activities that could naturally move outdoors in appropriate weather. Porches or terraces beside an important pathway or entry can serve as a transition area between the indoors and outdoors. Visitor and drop-off entries (in some situations) as well as entrances to the secured outdoor space can be natural places for informal visiting and viewing. Porches should be partially covered to provide protection from the weather.

6. *Sun room.*   A conservatory or sun room adjacent to the secured outdoor area can provide a place for viewing, visiting, planting and caring for plants, or sitting in the sun. It can be a natural transition to the outdoors. An aquarium with brightly colored fish can provide a positive, soothing sight for residents to watch.

Sun room.

Patterns of *enclosure* define the edges of a place. A garden with boundaries is somehow more comfortable than a garden without. Enclosure provides a garden with an inside edge. These edges may be building walls and windows, fences, garden walls, or plantings. An enclosure acts both as a shield and protector of those within its confines and brings comfort and security to people inside.

Subpatterns: Enclosure

1. *Gates, fences, and screens.* The design of gates and fences should be in keeping with the style of the building and surroundings. Trellised screens can help create comfortable pockets, protected from outside distractions, prevailing winds, and intense heat from the sun. Define the edges of the garden using plantings, screens, or fencing.

2. *Awnings and arcades.* Awnings and arcades can be used to screen direct exposure to harsh weather conditions such as sunlight, rain, snow, or wind and provide a covered place for walking. People need an in-between area to adjust to the outdoor light. An overhead canopy, porch roof, awning, or arbor will filter or shade the glare from bright sunlight.

Patterns that create and control *views* are essential to the quality of experience of observers. Views from within the garden are important to

Gates, fences, and screens.

Awnings and arcades.

create a sense of movement and passage through the garden. Some views are open and some filtered, some views frame vignettes and others look off into the distance, beyond the garden walls.

Subpatterns: Garden Views

1. *Distant views.*   Views out from the garden or long views within the enclosure of a garden expand the feeling of freedom and connection to the larger landscape.

2. *Inside views.*   Vignettes or small views within the garden help create the illusion of passage through and around the designed landscape. Views connect garden places.

3. *Filtered views.*   Use trees and trellised vines to create a quiet sense of enclosure without completely obstructing the views beyond.

4. *Forced perspective.*   Use plantings and structures to either shorten or lengthen views. Distance between plants or location can accomplish the illusion of either increased or decreased view distances inside or beyond the edge of the garden.

5. *Sight-line views.*   Strategically located along the paths and from indoors, make visual connections between places and activities to encourage movement into and throughout the garden.

6. *Vignettes.*   Use plantings or structures to create or frame views in the garden. Plantings with strong silhouettes are best used to frame distant views while softer branching structures can frame selected views inside of the garden from where people tend to sit. These captured vignettes help create a succession of experiences.

Distant views.

Inside views.

Filtered views.

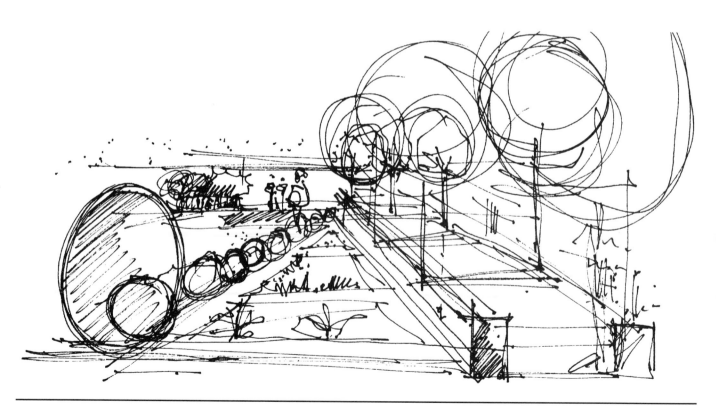

Forced perspective.

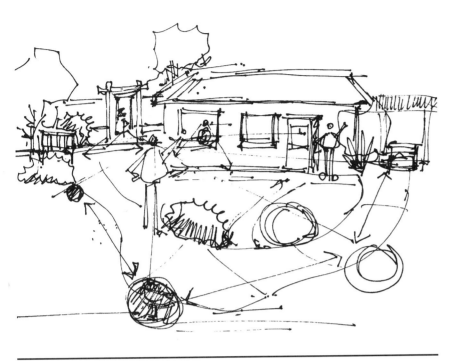

Sight-line views.

Vignettes.

Patterns that create form and give the dimension of growth and change to the garden are uniquely related to *plantings*. Plantings are what make the garden distinctive from an indoor environment. Plantings can be used to enclose, to frame, to soften, to enliven, to filter the sun, to clean the air, to provide homes for birds and creatures, and to invite nature into the lives of people.

Subpatterns: Plantings

1. *Framework plantings.*   Specimen trees accompanied by shrub masses or signature plants begin to create the living structure of the garden. Strategic placement and individual forms of plants are the foundation or framework for the other plantings and green space.

2. *Sunny places, arbors, and shade.*   Provide places for people to sit in the sun, under a canopy or arbor with vines for filtered sunlight. Plants and screens can be effective in filtering breezes and cooling in summer, or they can be comfortable pockets to extend seasonal use. For people who are more sensitive to temperature changes, the effects of cold or heat should be minimized.

Framework plantings.

Sunny places, arbors, and shade.

Evolving gardens.

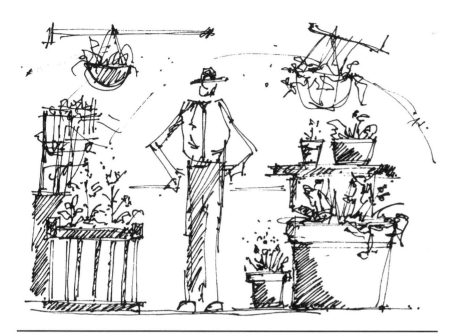

Container gardens.

Flower borders and window boxes.

3. *Evolving gardens.* Some gardens within the larger landscape are best when allowed to evolve over time. People need some place in the garden to create new combinations of plants; to bring plants from home, to grow vegetables and flowers.

4. *Flower borders and window boxes.* Brightly colored flowers in borders along pathways, in containers or window boxes, add personality and life to the garden. Use vibrant reds, yellows, and oranges to draw people into the garden. Softer hues (blues, pinks, and white) can be used in quiet areas and in shade.

5. *Container gardens.* Raising the level of plantings is an effective way to bring the garden closer to the observer. Containers of all styles, sizes, and materials can be used in situations where not much green space or open ground is available for planting. Containers can be moved to form enclosure, used as landmarks along pathways and at entrances, and provide small areas for individuals to plant and tend to with a minimum investment of money and time.

Furnishings provide a social dimension to the development of design patterns. People will use outdoor seating areas if there are adequate and inviting places to sit comfortably and enjoy the company of other people or views of the garden. Garden furnishings include tables, chairs, and accessories as well as sitting walls, sculpture, and minor water features.

Subpatterns: Furnishings

1. *Nomadic chairs.*   People want to move chairs and tables to suit their needs. Lightweight, sturdy chairs and other furnishings allow people to control their placement to take advantage of sun, shade, and shelter as desired. Use comfortable and sturdy but lightweight chairs and tables that can be arranged to create a friendly circle for family visits. The surface area should be spacious enough to arrange some chairs in a circle for larger group activities.

2. *Council ring.*   Create places for people to sit and talk or tell stories. Use permanent seating such as a seat-wall or benches in a circular form that are at a comfortable conversation distance for small groups of 6 to 10 people to gather. The ring can be complemented by moveable furniture.

3. *Structured seating.*   Fixed, strategic placement of some benches and seating areas along the pathways is necessary to assure appropriate locations. The furnishings help form the framework of the garden.

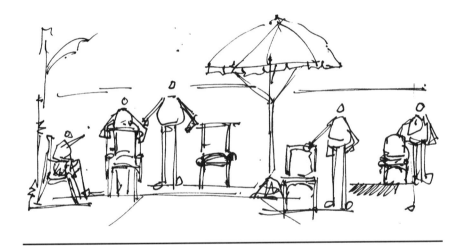

Nomadic chairs.

Structured seating.

The council ring.

Visiting alcoves.

4. *Visiting alcoves.*   Along pathways or as part of a larger gathering place, provide small alcoves for three or four people to visit. Use plantings or walls to make it a somewhat private, somewhat public place in the garden. Benches and chairs can be arranged to encourage conversation and visiting.

5. *Quiet places.*   Single benches along the pathway or in quiet areas of the garden provide a place for people to sit alone or with one other person. Create these places in areas where people can observe life in the garden.

6. *Sculpture and water features.*   Include sculpture or ornamental water features (e.g., birdbath, small fountain or waterfall, statuary) or a shallow basin for collecting rain. The introduction of water can provide places for birds to gather as well as bring an element of soothing sound to the garden. Fountains, reflective pools, and small fish ponds need to be carefully considered if used in these settings due to safety and occasional negative side effects for some people.

Patterns that direct way finding and orientation for people with impaired abilities to negotiate their surroundings can be considered *environmental cues.* Some elements of the garden can be used as cuing devices for residents or patients who suffer from some cognitive or physical impairment that prevents them from being able to negotiate their way completely through the garden. Particular types of plantings, strategic placement, culturally significant, or intuitive symbolic meaning attached to certain elements may also be included in the plan. These objects or compositions of objects cue people to different places in the garden, seasonal awareness, or movement along paths by their effect on individual and social behavior

Quiet places.

Sculpture and water features.

1. *Spring and summer garden.* Choose some springtime blooming trees, shrubs, wild flowers, and bulbs to enjoy after the long winter. Trees that offer summer shade and filtered sunshine and flowering shrubs can enliven the hot summer months.

2. *Autumn and winter garden.* Vibrant orange and yellow autumn colors, harvest plants, and falling leaves are reminders of the coming winter. Trees and shrubs with interesting bark that retain some fruit or berries, evergreens, and garden structures can add interest to the winter garden. Indoor plants and gardening can provide garden-related activities while the garden rests until spring.

3. *Songbirds and butterflies.* Use plants that attract songbirds and butterflies to the garden. Locate groupings of large fruiting plants away from pathways to prevent berries from falling on walks. (Some edible-fruit plants may be planted near paths.) Place some feeders or specimen trees near windows to encourage people to watch from indoors.

Spring and summer garden.

Autumn and winter garden.

Songbirds and butterflies.

4. *Kitchen garden.*   Every home needs a garden in which to grow vegetables, herbs, blackberries, and flowers outside the back door, near the kitchen. A kitchen garden (raised beds, planters, window boxes) is a practical way to bring the garden into the domestic realm of the home. Plant small fruits, herbs, and vegetables in containers or raised beds accessible to residents. Use the harvest in desserts, salads, or cooking.

Rabbit hutch and homes for the birds.

Kitchen garden.

Lilac groves and rose gardens.

5. *Rabbit hutch and homes for the birds.* Provide places for both domestic and wild animals to live in the garden. Often migrating ducks will nest in courtyards, and chipmunks and rabbits may find a home there also. A rabbit hutch or small doghouse for a resident pet can bring an element of spontaneity and life to the garden. Birdhouses of many types and styles often have cultural significance and bring particular birds to the garden.

6. *Lilac groves and rose gardens.* Particular plant fragrances have a powerful effect on the memory and recognition of time and place. Place groupings of fragrant plants along popular pathways (where people pass by often). Consider seasonal blooming times, prevailing breezes, sunlight, and visibility from indoors as well as from within the garden. These plantings, when used as cuing devices, can be organized to provide color, fragrance, and form throughout the seasons.

7. *Marlene's garden.* Provide places where people can display personal garden plants or ornaments collected from home. Allow residents freedom to alter the plan and add a personal touch. Often family members, patients, or staff will bring plantings to add to the garden. Flexibility in design should allow for this to occur.

Marlene's garden.

Applying the Patterns

Taking the patterns from descriptive concepts composed of words, to physical features requires both a knowledge of human behavior and the process of composing and building the landscape. We will first look at the theory of symbolic representation in the landscape and then at the composition of places to create a garden that supports both the social and physical needs of people who will spend time within its walls.

Compose the Design

To compose a landscape that reflects the poetry of design language, we will begin with the review of design theories which describe social and spatial structural systems of design.

In a review of his own "prospect and refuge" theory, Jay Appleton explains, "What I was looking for was a simple model which could relate the idea of preference to a typology of landscapes through the medium of the biological and more particularly, the behavioral sciences" (Appleton, 1984). While attending a lecture given by Professor Appleton in 1990, I took note of the complexity necessary to explain clearly what he referred to as "in effect, an extremely simple idea" (Appleton 1984). Appleton's work explores our emotional responses to landscape as subjective and symbolic associations, both *intrinsic* (natural) and *symbolic* (culturally determined). Art is full of symbolism—symbols that stand for something else—as often is the world around us. He gave the simple example of birds living in the habitat of a mature tree, a tree that stands for something else (i.e., an ancient oak symbolizing strength or continuity of life, not a home for birds). At the risk of being another who misinterprets the theory, one could say that the tree is in a sense both a prospect and a refuge. He makes further reference to symbolism in language by suggesting that the meaning of things occurs when we move from nouns (*mountain, valleys, ridges*) to verbs (*ascend, meander, overlook*). To illustrate *prospect*, he uses examples of *deflected view* where the viewer is somehow intent on finding out what is just around the corner or the *horizon* that leads us to speculate what lies beyond it. To illustrate *refuge*, he uses images of seeking sheltered places or meeting a place along a path that diverges into two paths leading to the woods. Again in his review of

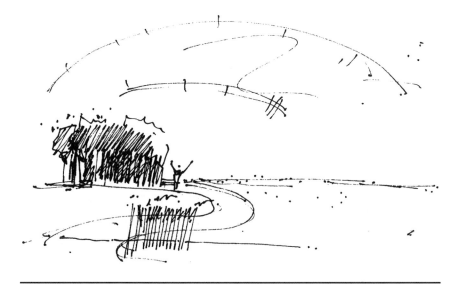

The sky as refuge.

the academic understanding of the theory, Appleton notes that landscapes do not necessarily need both opportunity for prospect and refuge to be satisfying or balanced. Very often the balance is more *potent* as a progression of experiences: "experiences of exposure to strongly contrasting landscape types, strong prospect, then strong refuge" (Appleton, 1984). These landscape types may include the use of voids and masses, light and shade, and enclosure and clearing. Even the dome of the sky becomes a refuge in contrast to darkness (Appleton, 1990).

This *complex-simplicity* is apparent in the work of many profound theorists in design and behavioral research (e.g., Alexander, 1979; Appleton, 1975; Lynch, 1960). "When the language is shared, the individual patterns in the language are profound. The patterns are always simple. Nothing which is not simple and direct can survive the slow transmission from person to person. There is nothing in these languages so complex that someone cannot understand it" (Alexander, 1979, p. 230).

The goal of this process is not to set out to test the theories (pattern language, imageability, prospect, and refuge) but to use them adapted to the design of landscapes for the purpose of healing. There is a single

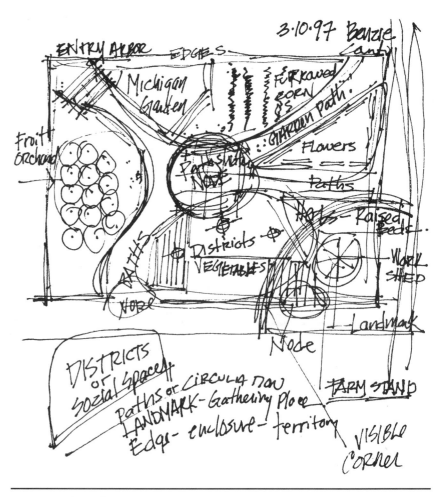

Patterns taking form.

common process that allows us to make buildings live, a precise process that cannot be used mechanically (Alexander, 1979, p. 12). There is a sequence of patterns and an order for fitting the patterns together. To allow the patterns and design to take form, you must give up control of the design and "let the pattern do the work" (Alexander, 1979, p. 398). You begin with one pattern and build upon the essential pattern elements, pulling-stretching the concept, minimizing or maximizing the intensity, until it fits the site and uses as it is best suited.

Each designed project is unique. The type of facility and therapeutic programs may determine design elements based on specific needs of patients/residents and staff. Conditions will vary. Local customs and architectural style, climate, and plant material, as well as the social and physical context in which the facility is set, will have an impact on the design solution. We form the design to suit users' needs.

When defining an environmental image and developing an understanding of the form of our environment, Kevin Lynch, city planning theorist, concludes that there are three formal types of image elements. The first is *identity*, an object or place that is distinctive from other things. *Structure* is the second element, which is defined as the spatial relation of the object to the observer. The third element, *meaning*, defines the significance, practical or emotional to the observer (Lynch, 1960).

Lynch further developed a system of elements that make up good city form. The five elements are paths, edges, districts, nodes, and landmarks. Each fulfills an essential function, and when they are put together, they create the fabric of the urban environment. The universal nature of the elements and the *complex-simplicity* of the theory allow the transformation or adaptation of the large-scale city planning to the more human scale of the landscape and the intimate scale of the garden. A *path* is in essence the "channel along which the observer customarily, occasionally or potentially moves." Seeing a path as more than just a linear corridor, Lynch also describes a path as a place: "Where the journey contains such a series of distinct events, a reaching and passing of one subgoal after another, the trip itself takes on meaning and becomes an experience in its own right (Lynch, 1960, p. 97). As it relates to the garden, the path is the lifeline of the garden as it is the vehicle for bringing people into and through the garden and with them, the social dimension.

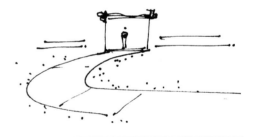

Path.

Edges are defined as linear elements or boundaries between areas. Edges can be "unifying seams rather than isolating barriers" and often are also paths (Lynch, 1960, p. 62). Edges in the garden can be elements that mark the perimeter of the garden (fences, hedges, walls) or that create separation between garden places (walkways, flower borders, trellis screens).

Districts are areas with a "strong image" and definite "inside and outside." Most often observers know the moment they arrive and leave a district simply by its distinctive character, although sometimes the boundaries are less certain (Lynch, 1960, p. 72). Within the garden setting, the patterns *working garden* or *front porch* are places identified by

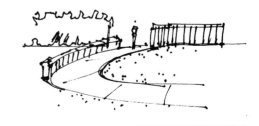

Edge.

District.

Node.

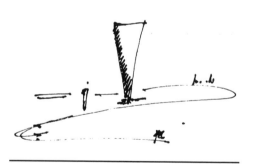

Landmark.

the familiar features, context, and form that are symbolic of their function (e.g., a potting bench or storage shed in the working garden or covered roof and low spindle railing enclosing the front porch). They have a strong sense of *meaning, structure,* and *identity.*

Nodes are symbolic of the place where old men sit outside of a small village post office or where young people gather on a popular street corner. They are "junctions and concentrations" or "connections of paths." Nodes can be outwardly reaching like a central plaza or inwardly focused like a small park hidden between buildings along a city street. A node in the garden is a *gathering place* or a crossing of paths where people pause—*a place to say hello.* A node can be a bench at the end of a garden path or a widened area in the walk that invites conversation between people passing by.

A *landmark* is a "point of reference." A landmark is a symbolic element that stands on its own. It is the feature that stands out from a "host of possibilities" that an observer will seek out for orientation (Lynch, 1960, p. 78). A landmark in the garden setting is most effective when used to identify the gateway or point of entry and departure from the building or as a central feature at the crossing of paths. When working with people who have some level of cognitive impairment, one primary landmark with significant secondary landmarks for leading people through the garden can modify the perceived length and complexity of larger path systems.

The scaling down of paths is accomplished by a "sequence of known landmarks or nodes along the path." Landmarks used to designate identifiable regions as a path enters and leaves them are a "powerful means of giving direction and scaling to a path" (Lynch, 1960, p. 55). A rose arbor over the entry to a small seating alcove or containers of strongly fragrant herbs and bright flowers are simple landmark elements to help people better negotiate their way around the garden.

However, Lynch cautions that "design elements are simply the raw material of the environment. They must be patterned together to provide a satisfying form" (Lynch, 1960, p. 83). When composing the design, you begin by defining the form and spatial nature of the individual patterns and develop the natural functional relationships between them. Following the methods laid out in *The Timeless Way* (Alexander, 1979), a composition formed using a pattern language has three required elements to define: First, define some physical features of the place that you choose to abstract. For example, the pattern *working garden* is a place where people do ordinary outdoor domestic work. That may include light gardening or yard work and possibly hanging out the washing. The second required element is to define a problem for which the pattern works to provide a solution. For example, there is no place for potting plants and working on outdoor projects or the opportunity to work outdoors. Third, to define a range of situations or contexts in which the pattern can occur. For example, provide space where people can work: a potting

Mrs. Olson hangs out the laundry, despite the threat of rain (Daniel Sjordal).

table and shelves, a place to sit down, storage for tools and soil, or a place in the sunshine for growing plants or hanging washing.

Returning to the basis of person-environment relationships, we begin to structure the design to facilitate the social functions, to associate patterns that work together, to define the composition by using the elements of form (path, district, edges, landmarks, and nodes) and fitting them to the site and building form.

Using the design objectives and pattern language as references, the next step in the process is to demonstrate their application to the development of alternative design concepts for a particular population (e.g., assisted living) setting. A physical description of a prototypical building and adjacent outdoor space remains constant. Three different design concepts are developed responding to a specific design objective. Residents have varied cognitive and physical ability levels; however, the home is intended to serve primarily ambulatory elderly residents with some minor cognitive deficits or physical limitations. The design should respond to the needs of all people who will eventually use the outdoor area, so universal design principles are implied. The building design is based on a single-family residential model. In developing the site-related criteria, we will set the residence in southern Illinois. The concepts are applicable to other climates; however, the siting issues will change depending on geographic location. The single-story residence borders the outdoor space to the north and west, and a privacy fence encloses the south and east sides of the yard. The doorways to the outdoor space are directly adjacent to a dining and activity area to the west and lounge to the north. Some resident rooms are south facing. The residence is located in the midwestern part of the United States; therefore, a southeast orientation was chosen to provide exposure to sun in the morning and early afternoon as well as protection from the northwest to lengthen seasonal use during fall and spring. A site analysis and behavioral-use analysis are necessary to begin forming a group of patterns for the desired project. The existing site documentation shows a worn concrete path connecting two existing doorways to the outdoor area. Areas that require special attention or repair are noted as well as microclimate limitations and opportunities.

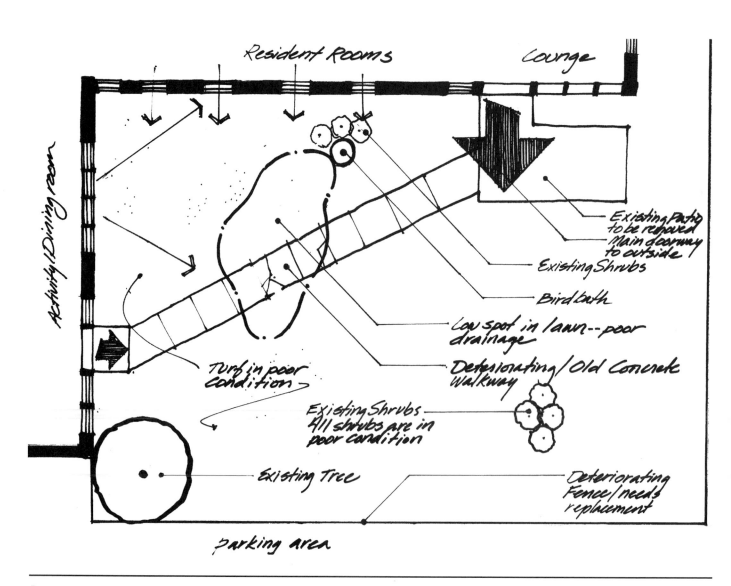

Document site conditions (Daniel Sjordal).

The behavior analysis is an example of how to document existing traces and patterns of use. Some physical features that may encourage or deter use are noted.

To reduce the incidents of unmonitored departures from the property, safety measures such as a privacy fence around the perimeter and windows with views of the outdoor space, were included in the design criteria. The outdoor space is intended to serve as a place for normal daily life events to happen involving residents, staff, and family members. Places for visiting, working, relaxing, and observing people or nature are provided for in the design concepts. Each concept emphasizes a particular design objective. Selected patterns are noted as well as additional descriptive annotations of intended design and patterns of use.

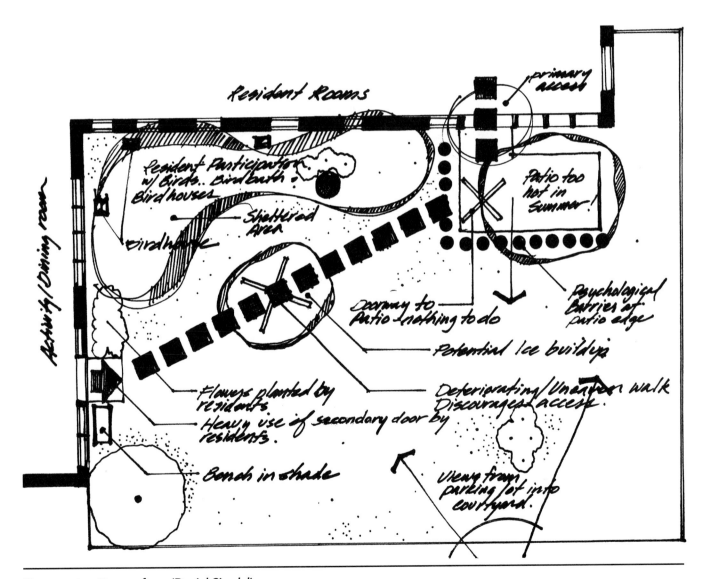

Document patterns of use (Daniel Sjordal).

Village Green Concept

- *Design objective*   Provide for safety and security.
- *Design patterns*   Sun porch, open lawn, lilac grove, quiet visiting alcove, wildflower garden, benches under the Juneberry trees, purple martin house, redbud grove, a home for the birds, sunny patio, flowering shrubs

The Village Green concept creates a traditional, parklike setting surrounded by pockets of activity, connected by a promenade or walking path. This concept is based on the idea that staff need maximum visibility of residents in the entire outdoor space. The layout is simple and offers staff and residents open views of the area from indoors and outdoors. Seating areas provide places for visiting in the sun room, alcoves, or on benches along the pathway.

The diagram gives a description of possible activities that may take place or be encouraged in the outdoor spaces. Residents have options to sit alone and observe (enjoying the sunshine) or actively participate in activities (planting marigolds). The simple layout provides security and ease of negotiability, while the other spaces provide places for interaction and involvement in everyday activities.

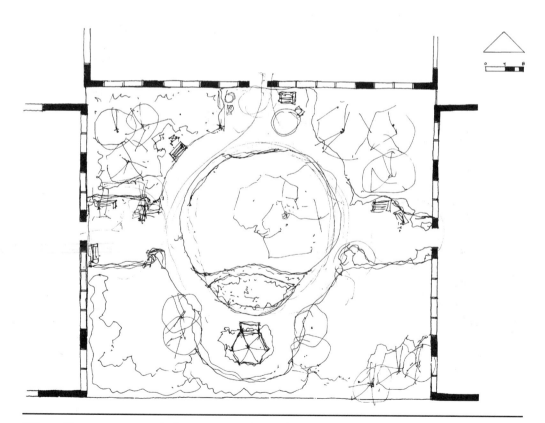

Village Green: compose design pattern relationships.

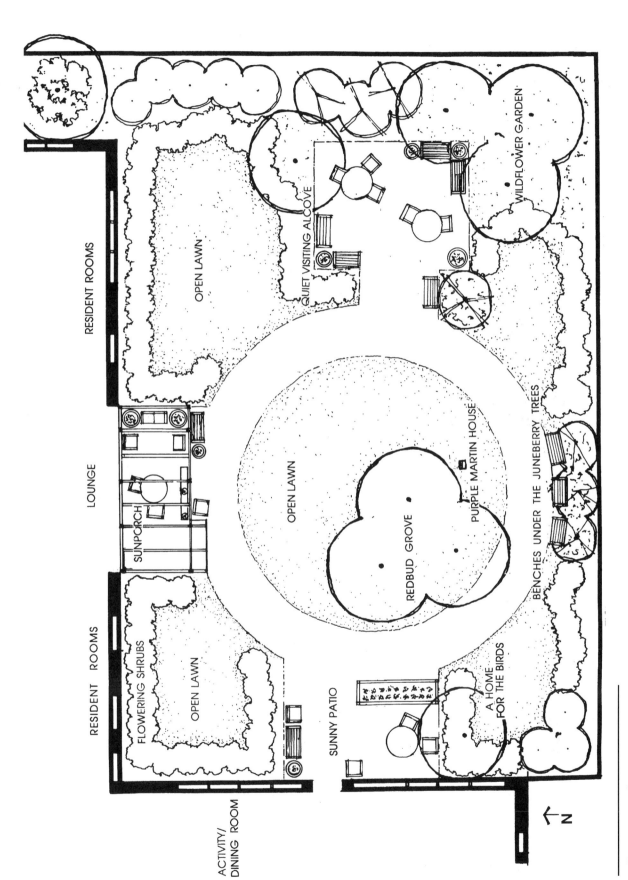

RESIDENT ROOMS

OPEN LAWN

QUIET VISITING ALCOVE

WILDFLOWER GARDEN

LOUNGE

SUNPORCH

OPEN LAWN

PURPLE MARTIN HOUSE

REDBUD GROVE

BENCHES UNDER THE JUNEBERRY TREES

RESIDENT ROOMS

FLOWERING SHRUBS

OPEN LAWN

SUNNY PATIO

A HOME FOR THE BIRDS

ACTIVITY/ DINING ROOM

N

Village Green: fit patterns to site.

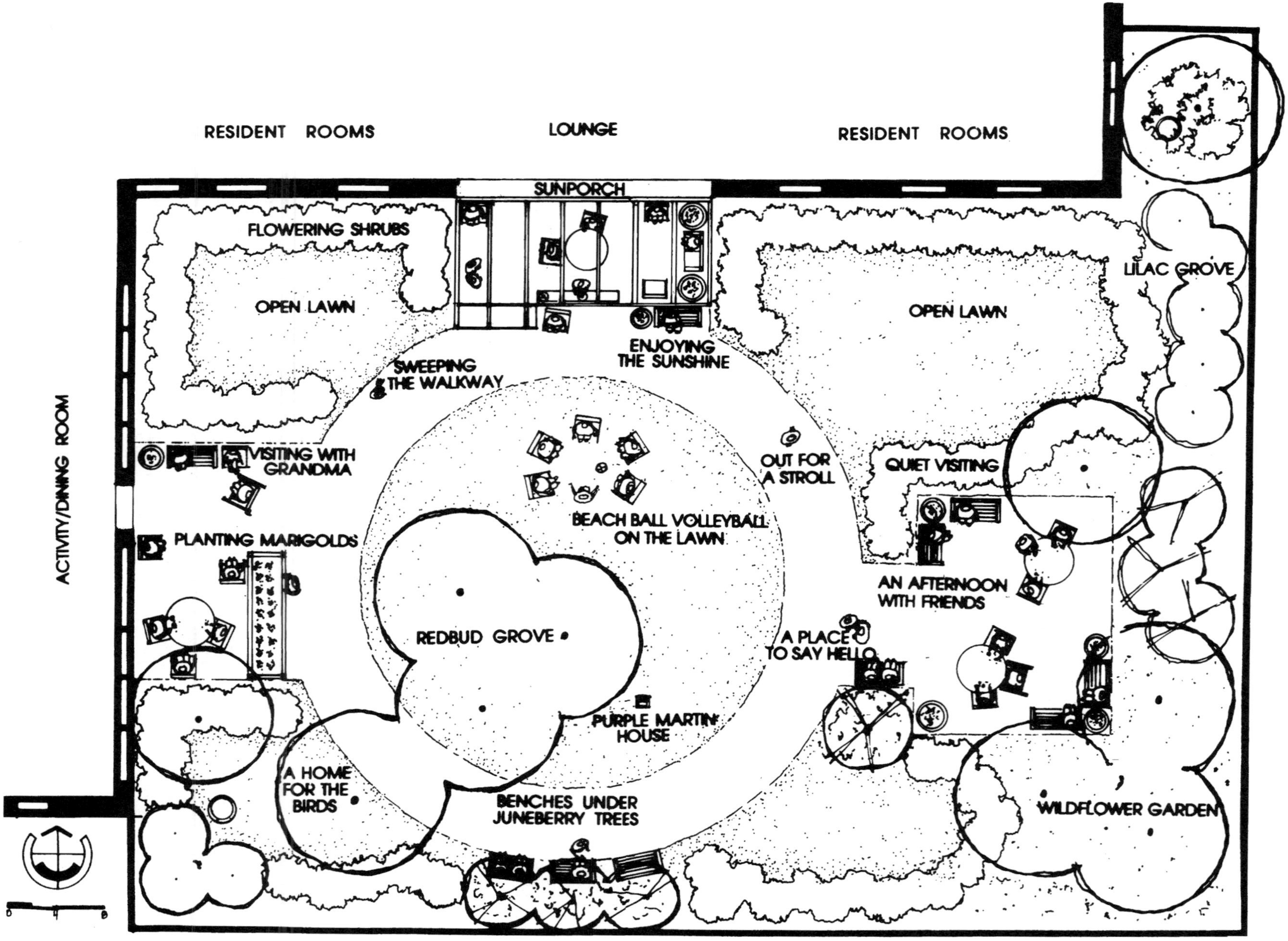

RESIDENT ROOMS

RESIDENT ROOMS

LOUNGE

SUNPORCH

ACTIVITY/DINING ROOM

LILAC GROVE

WILDFLOWER GARDEN

OPEN LAWN

QUIET VISITING

AN AFTERNOON
WITH FRIENDS

OUT FOR
A STROLL

A PLACE
TO SAY HELLO

ENJOYING
THE SUNSHINE

BEACH BALL VOLLEYBALL
ON THE LAWN

PURPLE MARTIN
HOUSE

BENCHES UNDER
JUNEBERRY TREES

SWEEPING
THE WALKWAY

REDBUD GROVE •

FLOWERING SHRUBS

OPEN LAWN

VISITING WITH
GRANDMA

PLANTING MARIGOLDS

A HOME
FOR THE
BIRDS

Village Green: intended patterns of use.

Garden Path Concept

- *Design objective*   Maximize spatial orientation.
- *Design patterns*   Sunny patio, lilac grove, a picnic in a grove of trees, white pine grove, quiet visiting alcove, purple martin house, birdbath, sun porch, Juneberry grove, a home for the birds, woodland path, flowering shrubs

This design emphasizes the intimate side of the garden. Small garden paths and landmarks are designed to invite movement through the garden. The concept is based on the belief that wandering may be the result of people searching for something or someone. The design is intended to allow residents the opportunity to freely walk in the garden and provides resting areas along the way. Benches, plantings, birdbaths, and gathering places serve as landmarks to improve orientation and encourage movement.

The design offers residents and staff a variety of places and opportunities to become involved with the natural environment and other people (a walk with Mrs. O'Leary). The design also provides separate alcoves for visiting (a quiet place) and single benches where residents can observe unobtrusively (squirrel patrol). The patio areas allow for group activities (an afternoon bridge party) or informal visiting (remembering the old days). The secondary pathway (woodland path) allows for solitude and retreat (waiting for the blue jay).

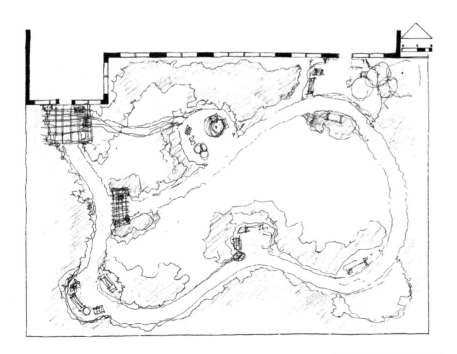

Garden Path: compose design pattern relationships.

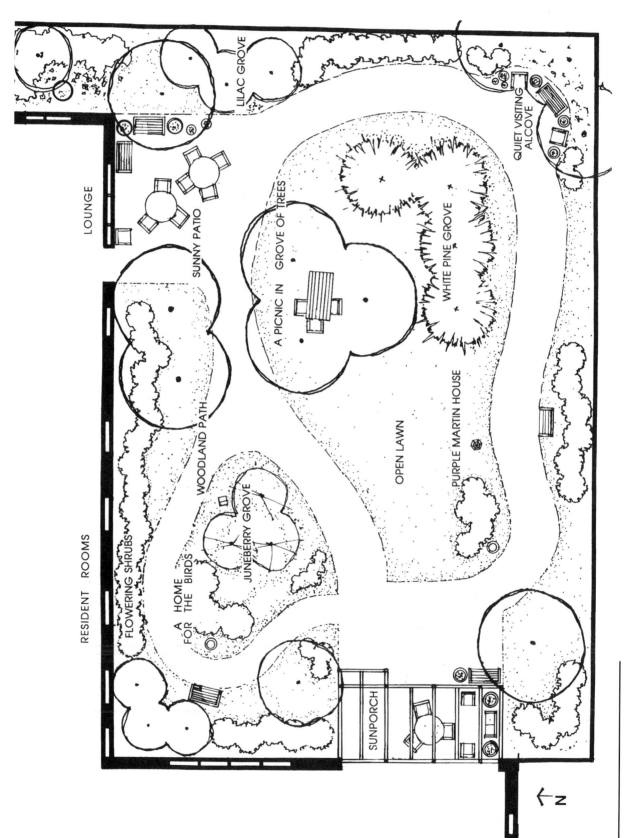

LILAC GROVE

QUIET VISITING ALCOVE

LOUNGE

SUNNY PATIO

A PICNIC IN GROVE OF TREES

WHITE PINE GROVE

RESIDENT ROOMS

FLOWERING SHRUBS

WOODLAND PATH

A HOME FOR THE BIRDS

JUNEBERRY GROVE

OPEN LAWN

PURPLE MARTIN HOUSE

SUNPORCH

N

Garden Path: fit patterns to site.

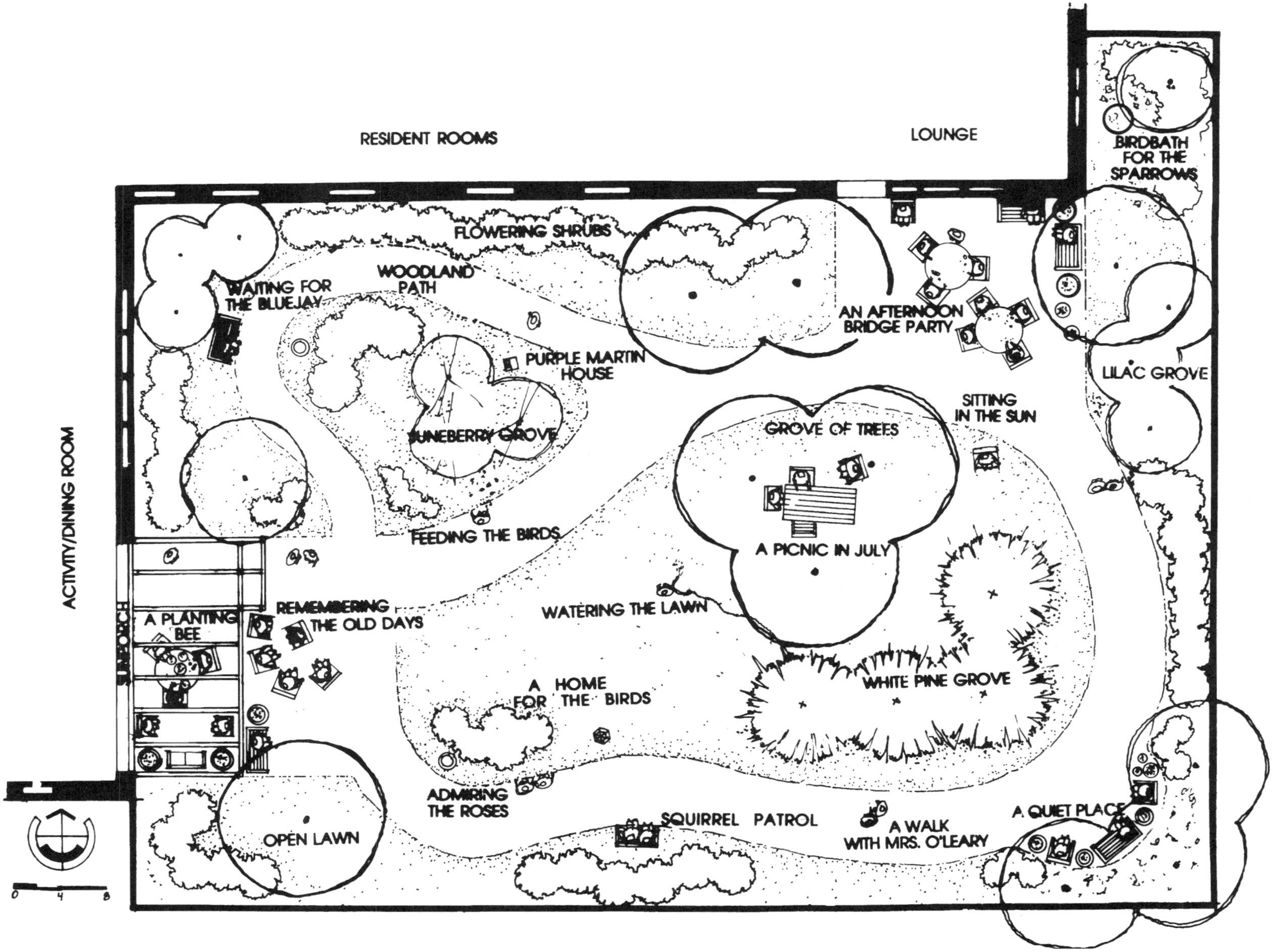

BIRDBATH FOR THE SPARROWS

LILAC GROVE

LOUNGE

AN AFTERNOON BRIDGE PARTY

SITTING IN THE SUN

GROVE OF TREES

A PICNIC IN JULY

WHITE PINE GROVE

A QUIET PLACE

A WALK WITH MRS. O'LEARY

SQUIRREL PATROL

RESIDENT ROOMS

FLOWERING SHRUBS

WOODLAND PATH

PURPLE MARTIN HOUSE

JUNEBERRY GROVE

FEEDING THE BIRDS

WATERING THE LAWN

A HOME FOR THE BIRDS

ADMIRING THE ROSES

WAITING FOR THE BLUE JAY

REMEMBERING THE OLD DAYS

A PLANTING BEE

OPEN LAWN

SUNPORCH

ACTIVITY/DINING ROOM

0 4 8

Garden Path: intended patterns of use.

Main Street Concept

- *Design objective*   Allow for a range of abilities.
- *Design patterns*   Sun porch, front porch, open lawn, woodland path, old-fashioned screened gazebo, Juneberry cove, a quiet place for visiting, garden path, lilac grove, flowering shrubs, rose trellis, open patio, purple martin house, tree grove in the open lawn, benches under a tree

The Main Street concept reflects the active social part of the garden. Residents with varied levels of ability are offered opportunities to participate in the outdoor activities. Areas near the entrances provide places to watch people coming and going without venturing too far from home. The main walking path and gathering areas promote informal visiting and participation. A smaller path and seating areas provide retreats for quiet visiting or observing from a distance.

The front porch can be a place for visiting with residents less ambulatory (quiet time with mother) as well as allow for passive participation from indoors. The sunny patio area is a place for people to garden (planting petunias), visit, or just sit near the entry. The central pathway and open lawn areas provide places for playing and walking for those less mobile and for quiet observation (pathway monitor). Residents who are more alert and active are provided more challenge with the more remote pathways (garden path, woodland path). Smaller alcoves are also provided for visiting away from the main activity areas (watching for Peter Rabbit).

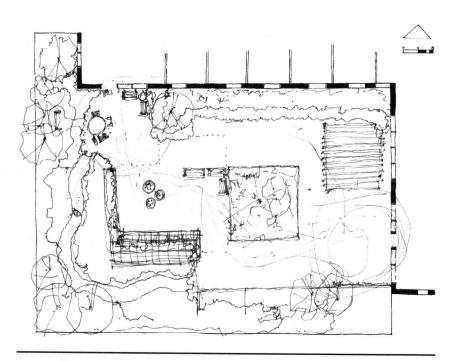

Main Street: compose design pattern relationships.

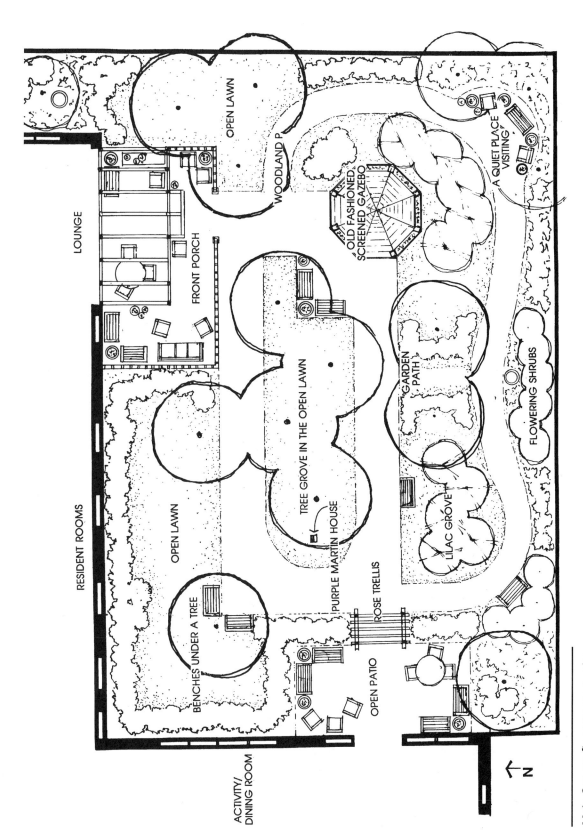

LOUNGE

RESIDENT ROOMS

FRONT PORCH

OPEN LAWN

WOODLAND P

OPEN LAWN

"OLD FASHIONED
SCREENED GAZEBO"

A QUIET PLACE
VISITING"

TREE GROVE IN THE OPEN LAWN

PURPLE MARTIN HOUSE

GARDEN
PATH

BENCHES UNDER A TREE

ROSE TRELLIS

LILAC GROVE

FLOWERING SHRUBS

ACTIVITY/
DINING ROOM

OPEN PATIO

N

Main Street: fit patterns to site.

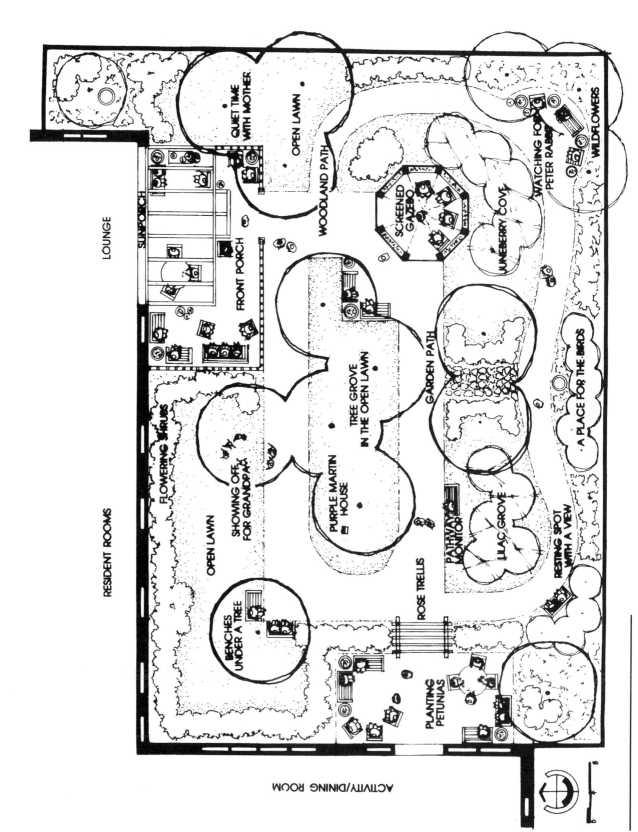

RESIDENT ROOMS

LOUNGE

SUNPORCH

FRONT PORCH

FLOWERING SHRUBS

OPEN LAWN

SHOWING OFF FOR GRANDPA

BENCHES UNDER A TREE

PURPLE MARTIN HOUSE

TREE GROVE IN THE OPEN LAWN

ROSE TRELLIS

PLANTING PETUNIAS

GARDEN PATH

LILAC GROVE

PATHWAY MONITOR

RESTING SPOT WITH A VIEW

A PLACE FOR THE BIRDS

JUNEBERRY COVE

SCREENED GAZEBO

WATCHING FOR PETER RABBIT

WILDFLOWERS

WOODLAND PATH

QUIET TIME WITH MOTHER

OPEN LAWN

ACTIVITY/DINING ROOM

Main Street: intended patterns of use.

Review and Refine the Site Plan

The layout of a design on a site requires an understanding of the concepts discussed in the three alternative concepts; however, it is more important to understand the life of the place and people for whom you are designing. "The mere use of pattern languages alone does not ensure that people can make places live" (Alexander, 1977, p. 229). Through the integration of the behavioral research techniques mentioned in Chap. 1, we can begin to formulate a design that functions as both a social space and a place of beauty. The intrinsic quality that creates a place that is healing to the mind, body, and spirit is that it is a "system" of elements that work together in a harmonious balance and support of people who enter inside. A *system of design* means that if you take out one of the parts, the system breaks down and no longer functions at its maximum potential (Zeisel, 1997). Our goal is to design landscape systems to support the ordinary daily life of people living in or spending time at facilities for the purpose of healing. Somehow, we must create places that are dynamic and alive with people and movement and contemplation and growth and change. Composing the patterns requires thought, and inquiry. Our questions, then, are, What is the something? Why is it helping to make the place alive? and When, or where, exactly will this pattern work? (Alexander, 1979, p. 249).

First, begin to gain an overview of the philosophy of care and daily activities that take place both indoors and outdoors if possible. With an understanding of the indoor life of a place, circulation patterns, use patterns, and resident, staff, and visitor interactions, you can begin to formulate a program of use for the outdoor area. Based on this program of use and observations of daily life, a preliminary concept and selection of patterns can occur. With the patterns in mind and the indoor program of use of adjacent areas to the outdoor space, the design will begin to take shape. Begin first with mirroring the indoor activities with like outdoor activities (e.g., indoor dining:outdoor dining, indoor sitting alcove:outdoor sitting alcove, private rooms:private gardens). Then extend these activities out into the site as they fit to the property and site conditions (e.g., sun orientation, vegetation, topography, available space). Then begin to follow the system of patterns given in the first part of Chap. 2: indoors and outdoors, paths and landmarks, garden places, enclosure, views, plantings, furnishings, and environmental cues. The following project examples describe various ways in which the elements have been implemented into designs. In following this path of design development, there is the dimension of investment from all people who choose to become involved. This is the intrinsic element that brings the sense of life to the patterns and leads to the creation of a place that is alive. Each project has different levels and needs for the investment of people; however, the essential feature that will set one garden apart from another is the continued use of and active growth and change that make a garden or landscape unique from any other built environment. It is a challenge to some and a joy for others. The landscape that will be a place of healing is, like the process of healing itself, a gradual progression over time, and often occurs more rapidly with the help and caring of other people along the way.

1. *Hearthstone Alzheimer Care* at New Horizons is located in Marlborough, Massachusetts. Formerly a convent and religious school, the facility was renovated to accommodate 45 residents in a three-story structure; the two upper floors are residential units, and the ground floor is a common dining and activity area directly adjacent to a secured outdoor garden. The Hearthstone garden reflects the life of the people and life indoors. The philosophy of care is reflected in the design of the facility: Everyday life consists of activities that take place either in the "back stage" or "front stage" of a home. Back-stage places include the kitchen and laundry, mud room, and back porch. Front-stage places include the foyer and formal living area and the dining room and parlor, with a hearth or fireplace as the unifying element between the two. The garden mirrors these events in the landscaped courtyard with the building edge as the defining indoor-outdoor connection (Zeisel, 1997).

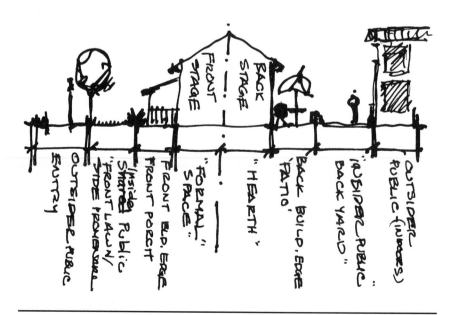

Sketch of Zeisel Residential Housing Model.

THE THERAPEUTIC GARDEN

OUTDOOR ENVIRONMENTS FOR PEOPLE WITH ALZHEIMER'S DISEASE

M.M. Tyson, Ageless Designs, Inc. 1995

ENVIRONMENT/DESIGN RESEARCH

- Although there is no cure for Alzheimer's Disease, it is possible to improve the quality of everyday life for people with the disease and their caregivers. Thoughtful planning and programming, combined with a calm, well-structured environment may help maintain the comfort and dignity of each person (Alzheimer's Association, 1990).

- Current Environment/Design research suggests that when integrated into the philosophy of care and program, the physical environment has the potential to play a therapeutic role in the care of older people and their caregivers (Calkins, 1988; Cohen & Weisman, 1990; Coons, 1988, 1991; Hiatt, 1986; Zeisel, Hyde & Levkoff, 1994). Familiar, home-like settings with views outside and direct access to a secured outdoor area may be especially beneficial to older people with Alzheimer's Disease (Cohen & Weisman, 1991; Zeisel, Hyde & Levkoff, 1994). Outdoor spaces, when designed to meet the specific needs of elderly people may provide opportunities to go outside and enjoy the social and scenic therapeutic benefits of the garden (Carstens, 1985, 1991; Loverting, 1990; Mooney & Nicell, 1992; Regnier, 1985, 1991, 1994). An appropriate design will respond to the needs of residents, staff and family/visitors as well as the indoor program and site conditions (Carstens, 1985, 1991; Regnier, 1985, 1991, 1994).

THERAPEUTIC GOALS

- We may take for granted our ability to do everyday things like set the table, feed the birds, water plants, find a sunny place to sit, observe chipmunks on the lawn, or simply enjoy the view through a window from indoors. These ordinary events may be reinforced through sensitive therapeutic programming and design. Therapeutic goals provide the framework within which the environment may be designed (Cohen & Weisman, 1991).

The specific needs of residents, staff and family/visitors are considered.

RESIDENTS

- Support abilities and compensate for losses
- Instill a sense of belonging and usefulness
- Provide opportunities to continue work, profession or hobbies
- Re-establish connections to the familiar
- Establish a sense of personal pride in surroundings
- Maintain a sense of security in physical surroundings
- Heighten awareness of nature, seasons, place and time
- Create places for physical exercise
- Maximize a sense of independence and freedom

STAFF

- Create a pleasant work environment
- Provide desired amount of space for activities
- Allow for complete surveillance of area
- Maintain flexibility to adapt environment to changing needs
- Provide places for resident respite from stressful situations
- Designate places for staff breaks and respite
- Provide ability to use space around the clock
- Establish pathway system to meet needs of wanderers

FAMILY AND VISITORS

- Provide assurance that residents have quality care
- Provide a familiar home-like living environment
- Offer opportunities for residents to continue normal social roles
- Create a sense of privacy and comfortable places for visiting

DESIGN GOALS AND GARDEN ELEMENTS

Design Goals and Garden Elements translate therapeutic goals into spatial forms and order the outdoor areas to bring about the desired responses of the people who will use them (Alexander, 1977; Lynch, 1960; Zeisel, 1977).

Provide Safe and Secure Outdoor Spaces for Residents

- Windows to observe
- Plant material
- Railings
- Garden walls, gates and fences
- Entryways to the outdoors
- Night-time lighting

Integrate Indoor and Outdoor Spaces

- Windows and doors
- Porches and verandas
- Conservatory/sun room
- From darkness to light
- Awnings and arcades
- Indoor and outdoor rooms
- Breezes and sunshine

Define Form and Character of Areas

- Gathering places
- Quiet "Away" places
- The working garden
- Visiting alcoves
- Open spaces
- Things from home

Establish a System of Pathways and Landmarks

- The promenade
- A place to say hello
- Just around the corner
- Strolling garden
- Events along the way

Heighten Sensory Awareness and Experience

- Lilac groves and rose gardens
- Flower borders and window box gardens
- The garden in winter
- Fountains and water features
- The kitchen garden
- Springtime, summer and autumn
- Sunny places, arbors and shade
- Songbirds and butterflies
- Rabbits, ducks and kittens

RESTORATIVE QUALITIES OF THE GARDEN

- Gardens, whether classified as aquarian, medicinal, botanic, historic or backyard vegetable plot, reflect the universal desire for human interaction with the natural environment (Kaplan & Kaplan, 1990; King, 1979; Lewis, 1990).

- We respond to gardens or natural scenes in different ways. Images are formed by experiences and memories of places we have visited, gardens cultivated and tended or parks and open fields played in throughout our lifetime.

ALZHEIMER'S DISEASE

- Memories are significant for a person with Alzheimer's Disease. Thoughts, images and responsive emotions that were once retrieved without a second thought, often are confused or incomplete...sometimes lost forever. While familiar faces and names begin to fade, vivid memories and experiences from the past are often perceived as present day events (Alzheimer's Association, 1990).

Research report of therapeutic goals, design objectives and patterns (Design Partners, Racine, WI).

THE THERAPEUTIC GARDEN

OUTDOOR ENVIRONMENTS FOR PEOPLE WITH ALZHEIMER'S DISEASE

M.M. Tyson, Ageless Designs, Inc. 1995

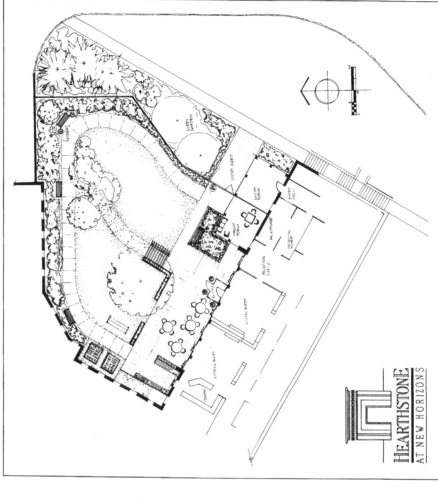

GARDEN DESIGN CONCEPT

The Hearthstone Garden Design is based on a residential model to define its character and organize outdoor spaces and places for everyday activities to take place (Zeisel, 1995).

The design incorporates environment/design research and informal interviews with residents, staff and family members conducted at the Hearthstone Garden site in Fall, 1994.

Some comments include:
* storing plants, pots along the edge
* a place to sit in light rain
* raking leaves with father
* fresh lilacs in spring
* throw seeds for birds on the snow
* a quiet place to rest
* vegetable garden...we will enjoy eating them
* a work table or bench with water source
* a place to get dirt on your hands – and no one cares
* lighted paths and trees
* a garden swing
* victory gardens

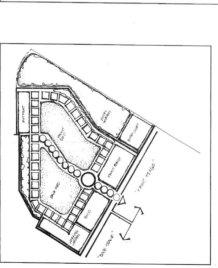

Design concept for Hearthstone at New Horizons (Design Partners, Racine, WI).

A single entry is located adjacent to the living area; however, a careful placement of garden features creates a sort of front-door–back-door entry to and from the garden. The primary patterns are front porch, front lawn, park, working garden, back patio, promenade, garden path (short-cut), fence enclosure, edge plantings, and framework plantings.

This process was unique in that the residents themselves were interviewed and shown a scaled model of the courtyard to gain individual impressions of the project before construction began. The process proved successful and was an essential factor in the atmosphere of continued involvement of residents, staff, and family in the life of the garden. The progression of plan composition moves naturally from indoors to outdoors and then from the building edge out to the garden.

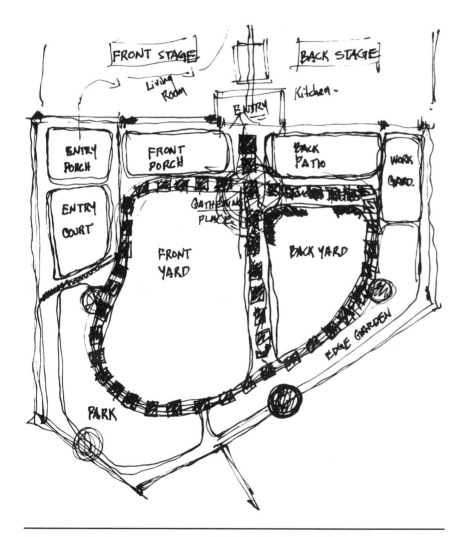

Compose the design patterns to fit inside site boundaries.

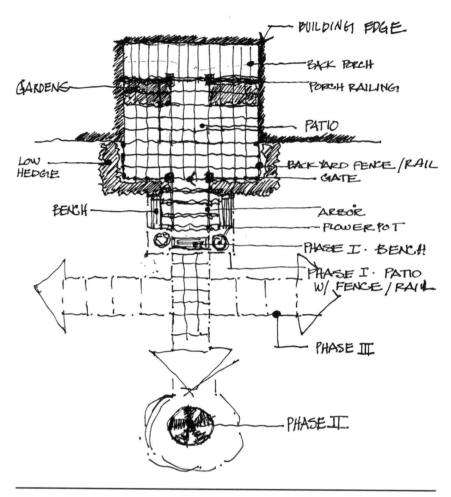

Create a path to move from indoor places to outdoor places.

Primary patterns begin to give form and definition of character to the places. The sequence of entry experience involves passing through both the doorway alcove and adjacent front-porch patio.

An entry serves as an arrival gateway.

A front porch is a doorway to the garden.

The progression of garden places leads to the front yard, park, and back around to the back yard, working garden, and back patio.

A front yard functions as a display place.

A retreat or park is a faraway place off the main promenade.

A back patio is a place to drink lemonade and talk.

A garden is a place for potting plants.

A backyard is a place to do work.

The use of edges serves several purposes in the garden setting. Edges can be used to separate activities or create definition or set boundaries for spaces.

Edges can create separation of places.

Edges can be paths between places.

Edges can create inside and outside boundaries.

Pathways can be considered edges but are most effective for way finding and bringing people out into the garden. Paths can go around, through, beside, and across garden places to create a sense of movement and provide varied experiences along the way.

A promenade is a wide path for walking and talking.

A backyard path goes across the lawn.

A front yard path means just passing through.

Reference landmarks along the pathway help to make the experience more interesting and assist people who may become disoriented. Reference landmarks can be small sculptures or planting areas while a primary landmark should be noticeably more significant than any other.

Reference landmarks are signposts along the way.

Benches are welcome landmarks along the path.

A landmark arbor is the Sears Tower of the garden.

Placement of and relationships between patterns are unified by paths and carefully defined edges. Exploring the relationship between indoors and outdoors to create familiar places and transition into garden is one way to begin formulating a composition for design.

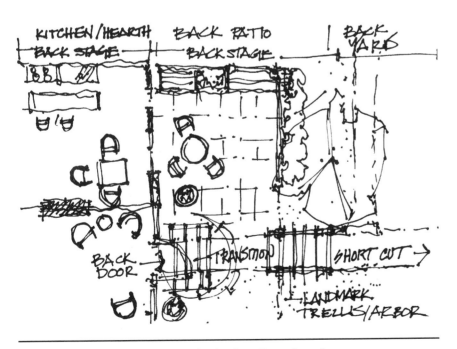

Kitchen and hearth reflected in the back patio and yard.

A garden path is a place to stroll.

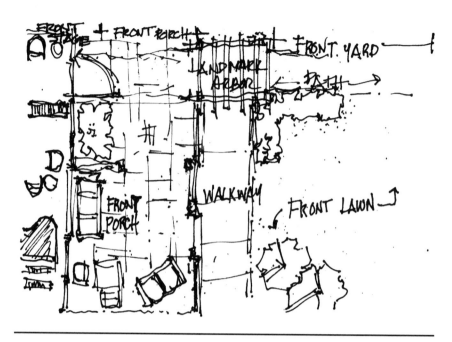

Foyer and parlor reflected in the front porch and yard.

Other areas in the garden that require special detailing may be created and then connected by the use of the path system, landmarks, and edges that both form and enclose them.

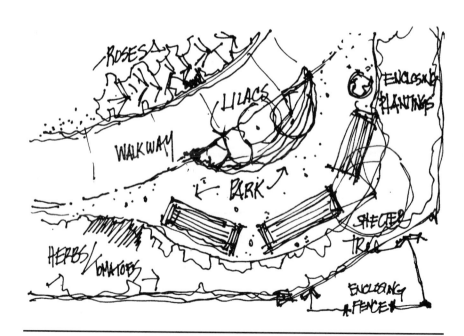

A park is a gathering place along the promenade.

To further test design theory, it is helpful to overlay annotated plans of the design principles in order to check the design before building begins.

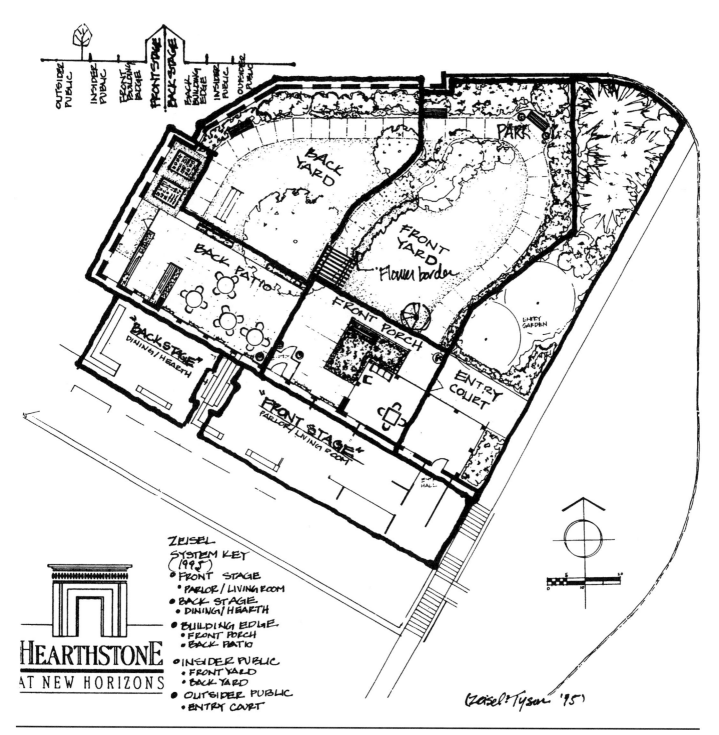

Overlay of Zeisel design program to check design.

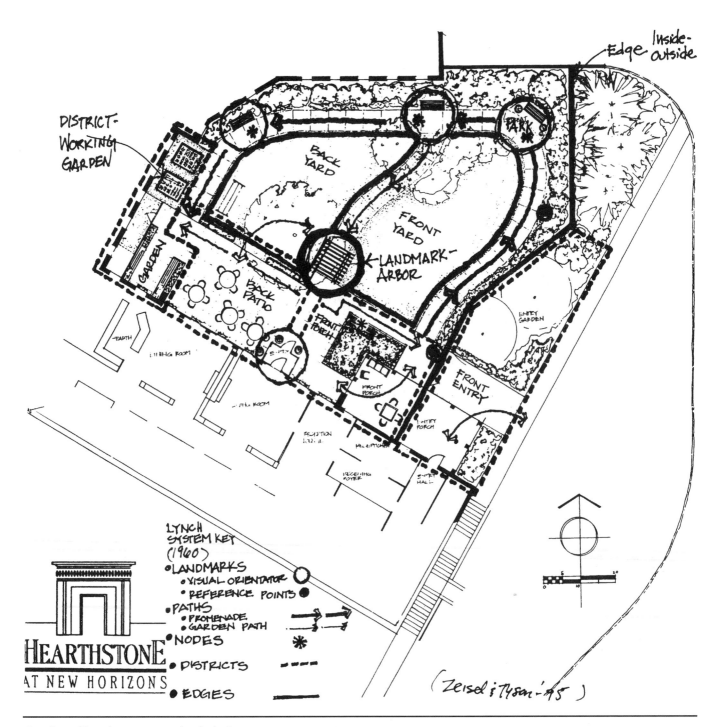

Overlay of Lynch system to check design.

The process of installation is part of the therapeutic benefits to patients or residents; therefore, it is important to keep in mind that the progression must take place over a period of time in order to be effective. During construction it is worthwhile to take note of behavior changes and interaction with people working outside. Changes often are necessary during the process, which may be a reflection of how spaces are actually used and may be better designed. A finished product is never finished. Evaluation and testing bring new knowledge and constant revisions to improve the place and level of use.

The Hearthstone garden site before construction.

The back door/front door entry from outdoors.

Inside looking out from the hearth (John Zeisel).

Inside looking out from the parlor (John Zeisel).

Bird's-eye view of the garden (John Zeisel).

Stepping out to check the weather.

View from the back patio to the park.

The entry arbor and field stone wall are gateways to the garden.

Garden sculpture as a reference landmark along the way.

The open wall creates a short-cut path across the lawn.

Direct pathway with an attainable destination.

View from park back to front porch and entry.

The ladies check up on new plantings (John Zeisel).

The garden path as a connector between places (John Zeisel).

Strolling home (John Zeisel).

2. *Hearthstone Alzheimer Care* at Heights Crossing is located in Brockton, Massachusetts, and is a second Hearthstone garden. It follows a similar concept of indoor and outdoor image and activity reflection. The facility itself is smaller, and the garden is quite a bit smaller as well. The principles of back stage and front stage have been incorporated into a mini-Hearthstone at Marlborough garden.

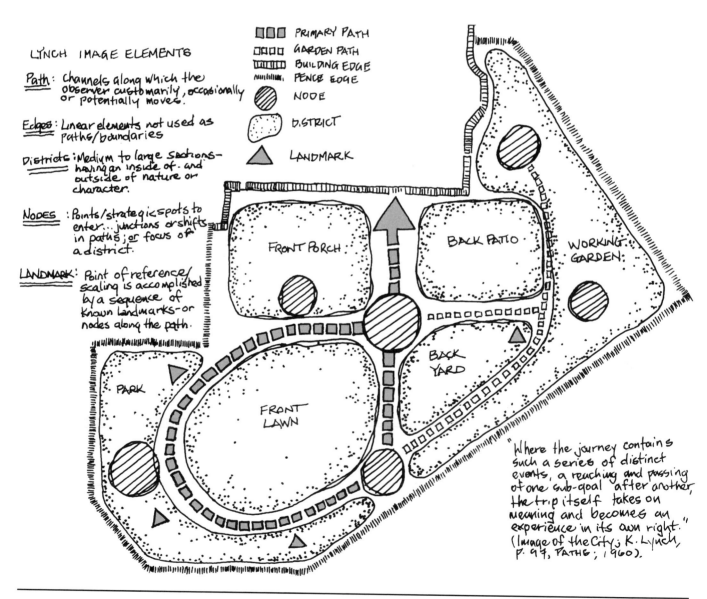

Applying Lynch principles to the Hearthstone garden at Heights Crossing.

The primary landmark remains an arbor structure at the entry node. A pathway connects the front porch, park, and back patio and the working garden. A short-cut or garden path dissects the lawn area to create an edge of front yard–back yard as in the other garden design. A small picket fence and arbor gate mark the entry into the back-patio area and give a sense of separation and privacy to residents.

The park is a small sitting alcove located at the farthest point from the main entry to create an away feeling for people resting there.

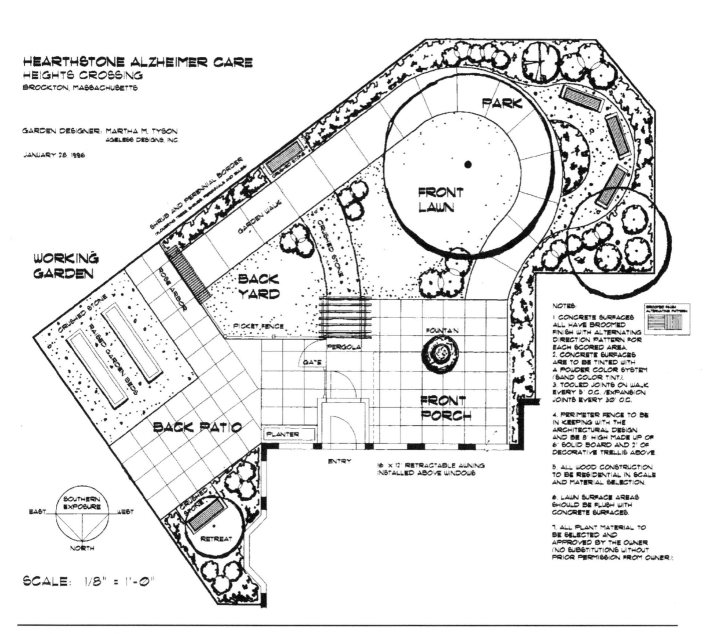

Hearthstone Heights Crossing: fitting the patterns to the site.

The garden is under construction at the time of this writing. Future residents will be encouraged to call the garden their own and will be invited to participate in gardening programs and individual planting projects as well. The design can be tested and checked by using overlays of intended use and theory.

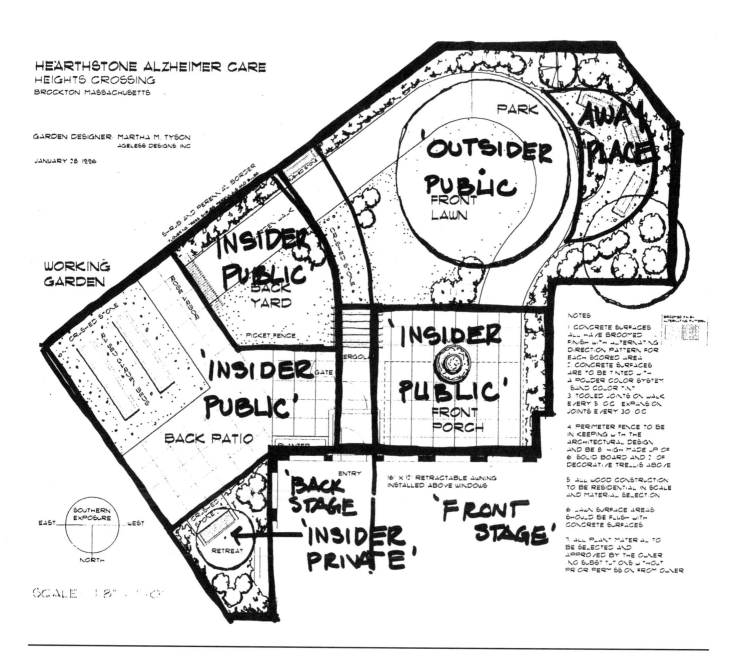

Overlay of Zeisel model to check design.

The model of Lynch's system of elements helps to clarify and solidify the principles of the design. This checking of the design and function before construction is useful in ensuring the most appropriate design solutions and fit to the intended social program.

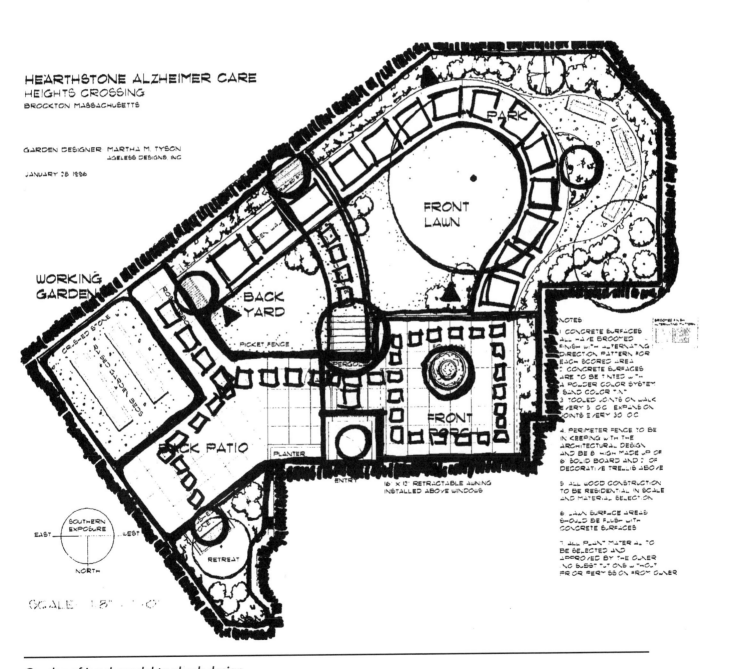

Overlay of Lynch model to check design.

Alexander's patterns reflect and refine the character and intended use of the garden. The shared patterns and relationships between patterns create the atmosphere, both social and physical, for the garden.

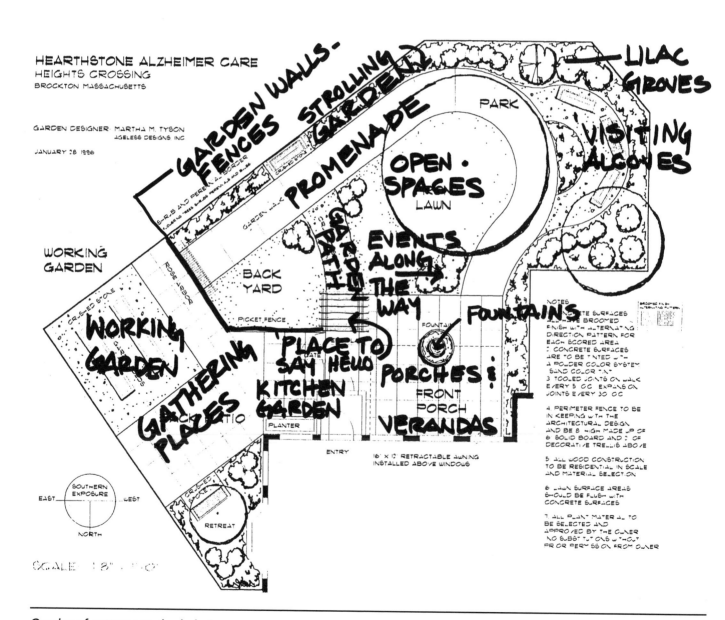

Overlay of patterns to check design.

3. *Lodi Good Samaritan Center* is a long-term-care facility located in Lodi, Wisconsin. Lodi is set in the countryside of the Wisconsin River valley just north of Madison, Wisconsin. The facility has several courtyards and outdoor spaces for residents, although the construction of a new Alzheimer's Care Unit provided an opportunity to adapt an already-existing enclosed courtyard for resident use. The history of the grounds and gardens shows that the use of outdoor spaces and gardening has been a part of resident daily life. The activity room and chapel overlook a gently rolling corn field planted and harvested every spring and summer. The existing courtyard needed renovation of pathways and concrete patios that were settling and breaking up. With the investment of staff and volunteers, a plan was drawn to meet the specific needs of residents from the Alzheimer's Care Unit and other residents, staff, and family as well. Residents of the home are invested in the grounds and upkeep of gardens and are looking forward to a place where they can go outside and walk, watch birds, and enjoy the sunshine. Construction began in the spring of 1997.

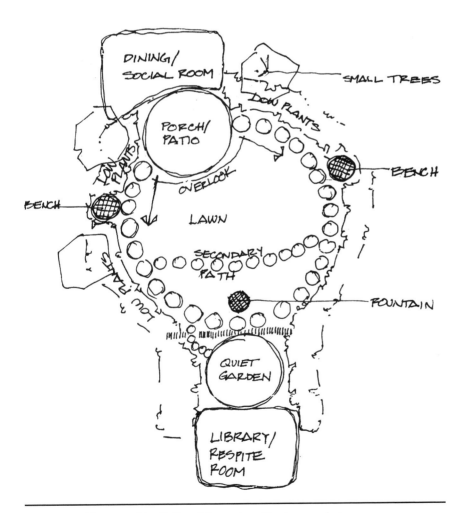

Conceptual layout of Lodi Good Samaritan Center garden.

The primary elements of the design are the pathway around a central grassy area with plantings of shrubs, small trees, and perennials underneath resident windows along the pathway. The pathway configuration provides small reference landmarks to ensure way finding and security for confused residents.

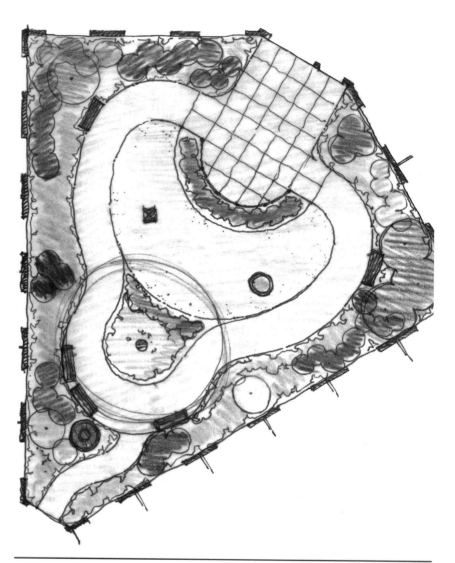

Fitting the patterns to the site.

Visibility is open from all surrounding residents' rooms and the library at the far end, which is accessed by a hidden service path. A primary patio and shade structure will provide a place for residents to walk freely outside from the indoor activity room. Plants were chosen for their "second-use" qualities to be used in arrangements or craft projects for the residents. The seasonal display of fragrance and color will bring a new life into the courtyard for all to enjoy. In the first phase of the project, the hard surfaces will be installed and other construction work will be accomplished. Large plantings will be installed by professional landscape contractors, and the final detail plantings of perennials and small shrubs will be completed by volunteers and residents in the spring.

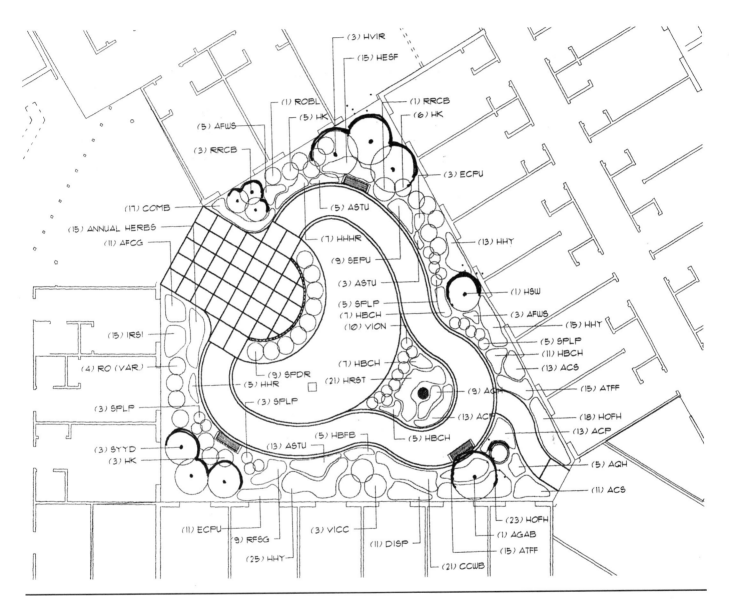

Refining plan for construction.

These project descriptions give an overview of the process and examples of how the process has different levels and types of involvement from residents or patients, staff, architects, and family members. Each project takes on a life of its own and with the investment of people, lives on far beyond those involved in the initial planning and planting. The next chapter brings the process of building into the therapeutic realm of creating healing gardens. The design and theory are in a sense the framework of a place that supports therapeutic opportunities and enhances both social and individual benefits.

Build

In the collections of Christopher Alexander, traditional methods of building and constructing have been synthesized that appeal to the sense of intuitive order and hierarchy of activities which take place in built environments. According to Alexander's principles, "There is a definable sequence of activities which are at the heart of all acts of building, and it is possible to specify, precisely, under which conditions these activities will generate a building which is alive" (Alexander, 1979, p. 10).

I repeat this from an earlier chapter to emphasize the underlying distinction between places that are *static and dead* versus *active and alive*. The application of these ideas to the creation of landscapes adds a dimension of continual growth and change that is unique to the natural world. In combination with the built environment—its connection to the constructed outdoor environment and nature—we begin to see how a discussion between a landscape that is alive and a landscape that seems dead can occur. One way to bring life to a project is through design patterns that respond to and enhance the social functions of the place. Another way to bring life to a project is to invite people to participate in the process of building.

1. The *Family Life Center* is a nonprofit agency that cares for people with dementia in the local Grand Rapids, Michigan, Community. The facility is a renovated Cloistered Convent, giving the garden and building a unique character, which is advantageous for the garden since it needs to be secured. The 8-foot brick cloister wall originally surrounded the entire grounds; however, with renovations and parking, a combination of wrought-iron fencing with pillars is in keeping with the original style and still provides needed security. The garden is designed for the specific needs of those with memory disorders. Each area integrates research, purpose, activity, and pleasure to create a place for the enjoy-

Springtime planting day.

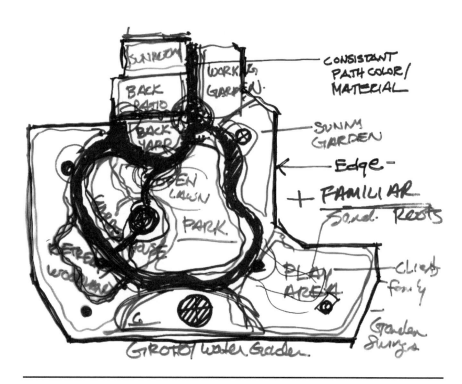

The Family Life Center garden is a collaboration of people in a plan sketch.

ment and enrichment of the entire family. The intended purpose of the center is to focus on the need for education and support of people in the community who are caring for older people with dementia. The garden is to be a place for the family, community, and day-care participants to be together in a comfortable and familiar setting. The garden project has been a collaboration between the local botanic garden; university students and faculty; and local garden clubs, designers, and nursery growers.

This collaboration is in keeping with the original spirit of the Family Life Center as a place for coming together. Fund-raising efforts involving national celebrities and local professionals have provided the necessary funding set aside for construction of a large portion of the plan. Most of the material and labor will be donated by local business people who have been very generous and supportive of the center's mission. At the time of this writing, the garden is not yet under construction.

The garden's pathway is its most important feature. The paths ameliorate confusion and promote security and sense of direction, and they are designed to invite people into the garden and lead them through it. The primary landmark is a centrally located arbor structure, which is the gateway to and from the garden. A garden house will be built as a secondary landmark and gathering place out in the park area of the garden. Secondary landmarks are strategically placed along the pathways to provide recognizable reference points. One of the major structural features

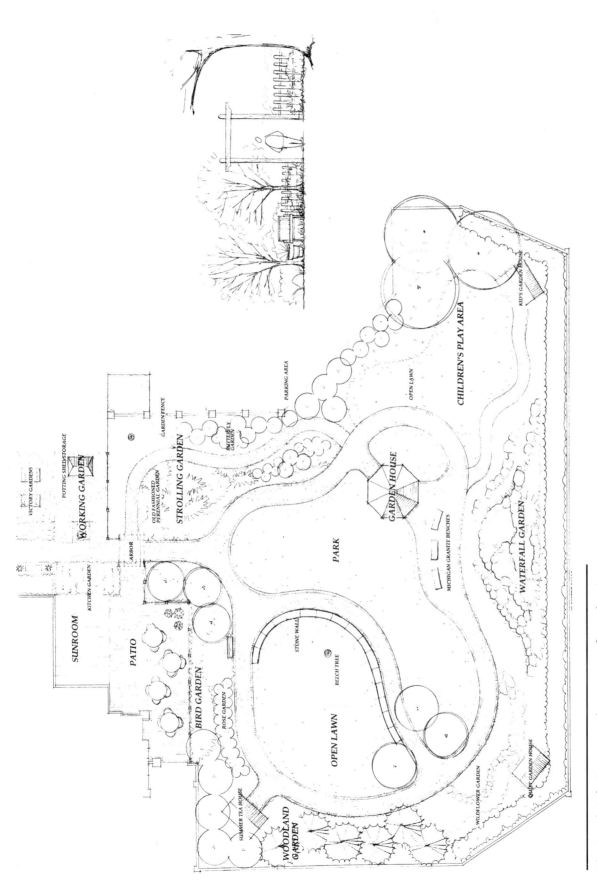

The Family Life Center garden patterns fit to the site.

VICTORY GARDENS

POTTING SHED/STORAGE

WORKING GARDEN

KITCHEN GARDEN

SUNROOM

PATIO

BIRD GARDEN

ROSE GARDEN

WOODLAND GARDEN

SUMMER TEA HOUSE

OPEN LAWN

STONE WALL

BEECH TREE

PARK

OLD FASHIONED PERENNIAL GARDEN

STROLLING GARDEN

BUTTERFLY GARDEN

ARBOR

GARDEN FENCE

PARKING AREA

GARDEN HOUSE

MICHIGAN GRANITE BENCHES

OPEN LAWN

CHILDREN'S PLAY AREA

KID'S GARDEN HOUSE

WATERFALL GARDEN

WILDFLOWER GARDEN

QUIET GARDEN HOUSE

of the garden is the conservatory. The conservatory, donated by a local businessperson and chair of the Garden Campaign, will open up the center's dining area and provide a year-round view of nature. From within the enclosure of the conservatory, participants will be able to relax and enjoy the sights of birds feeding, rain falling, flowers blooming, and snowflakes glistening. Winter use of the garden will be considerably increased in this northern climate. Night lighting along the paths and up lighting in specific trees will provide a place to go with family members or participants later into the evening hours. The garden is slated for construction in the spring of 1998.

The Family Life Center before construction.

Eight-foot cloister wall and service gate.

Meditation houses to be renovated as garden sitting places.

Existing remains of the cloister garden at the waterfall garden.

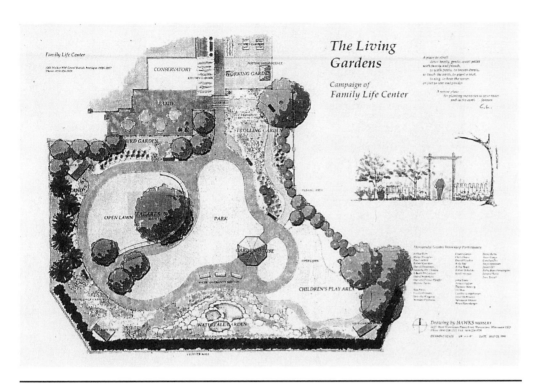

Family Life Center illustrative plan (designed by Martha Tyson/John Klatt/Gary Urban, The Hawks Nursery Company).

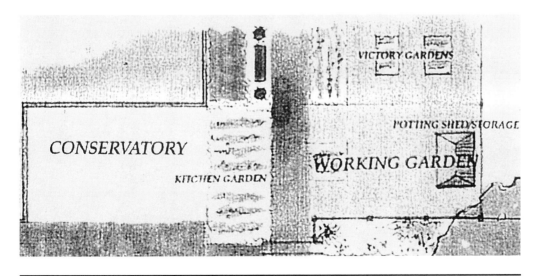

Conservatory and working garden.

Fabares beech tree in the open lawn.

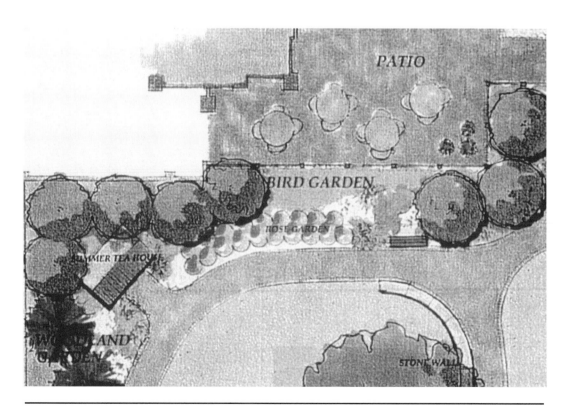

Patio and bird garden.

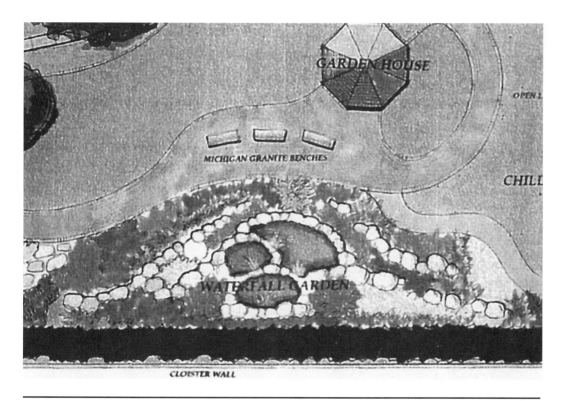

Renovated grotto creates the waterfall garden place.

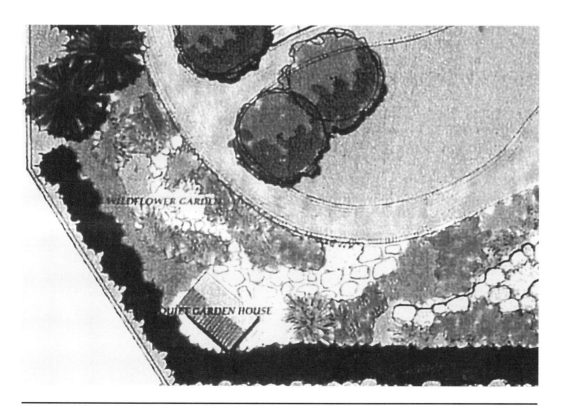

Michigan woodland garden along the path.

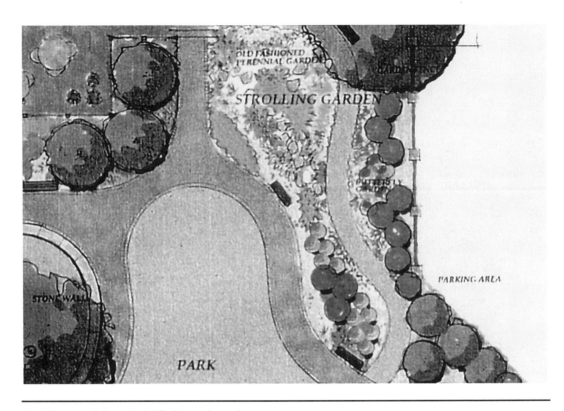

Strolling garden and old-fashioned garden.

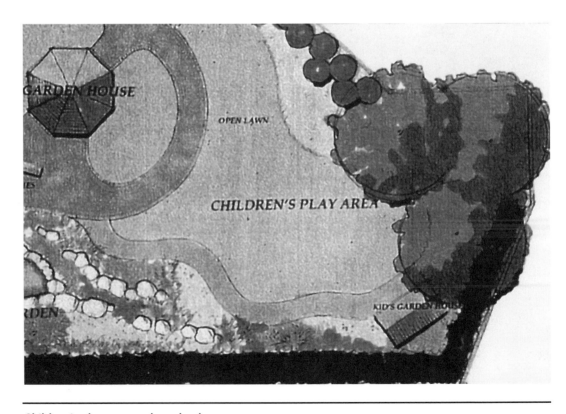

Children's play area and garden house.

2. The *Helen Bader Alzheimer's Center,* Milwaukee Jewish Home, Milwaukee, Wisconsin, is the realization of the dream of Mrs. Helen Bader of Milwaukee, Wisconsin. Designed to provide a homelike environment for people who suffer from Alzheimer's disease, the Helen Bader Center is home to residents of the Milwaukee Jewish Home and Care Center. The program encourages residents to continue with normal social roles and activities of everyday life. Dedicated staff and a directed activity program provide residents the support they need to maintain and continue with normal daily life activities and routine. The garden is an extension of the life indoors, providing residents the opportunity to step outdoors onto an enclosed rooftop patio.

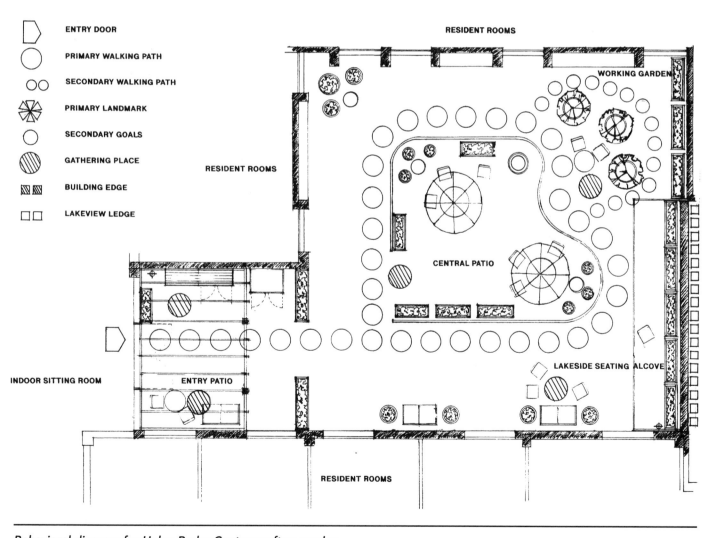

Behavioral diagram for Helen Bader Center rooftop garden.

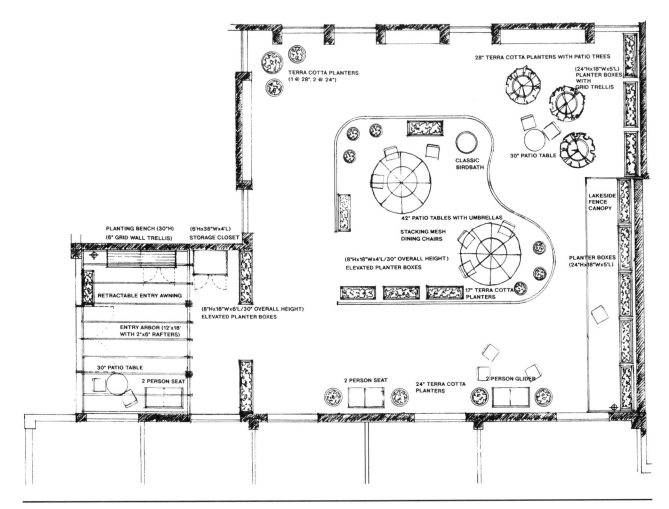

TERRA COTTA PLANTERS
(1 @ 28", 2 @ 24")

28" TERRA COTTA PLANTERS WITH PATIO TREES

(24"Hx18"Wx5'L)
PLANTER BOXES
WITH
GRID TRELLIS

30" PATIO TABLE

CLASSIC
BIRDBATH

LAKESIDE
FENCE
CANOPY

42" PATIO TABLES WITH UMBRELLAS

STACKING MESH
DINING CHAIRS

PLANTING BENCH (30"H)
(6" GRID WALL TRELLIS)

(6'Hx36"Wx4'L)
STORAGE CLOSET

PLANTER BOXES
(24"Hx18"Wx5'L)

(8"Hx18"Wx4'L/30" OVERALL HEIGHT)
ELEVATED PLANTER BOXES

RETRACTABLE ENTRY AWNING

(8"Hx18"Wx6'L/30" OVERALL HEIGHT)
ELEVATED PLANTER BOXES

17" TERRA COTTA
PLANTERS

ENTRY ARBOR (12'x18'
WITH 2"x6" RAFTERS)

30" PATIO TABLE

2 PERSON SEAT

2 PERSON SEAT

24" TERRA COTTA
PLANTERS

2 PERSON GLIDER

Layout plan for Helen Bader Center rooftop garden.

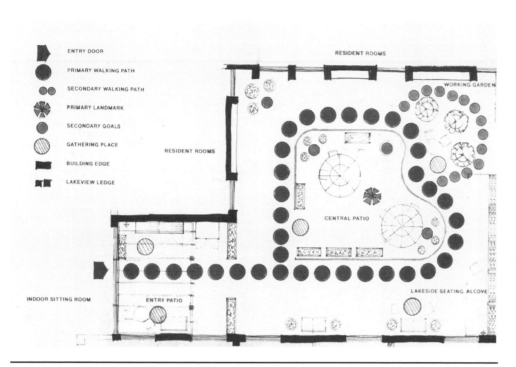

Primary path and landmark system.

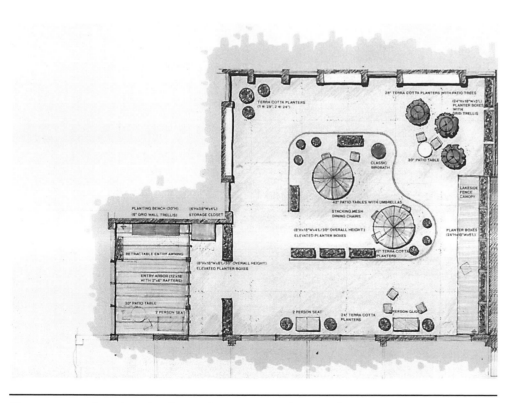

Illustrative garden plan of Helen Bader Center garden (Martha Tyson/Gary Urban, The Hawks Nursery Company).

Entry doors open to rooftop before construction.

With views onto Lake Michigan, this garden helps to maintain a connection to the natural world from a distance, and planting benches, container gardens, and raised window boxes allow for hands-on experience with planting and tending flowers, vegetables, and herbs. Awnings and umbrellas provide necessary shade during the heat of summer. Tables and movable chairs offer residents the freedom to sit and visit where they choose. Families enjoy the patio garden as well, for outdoor lunches, afternoon visits, and visiting with small children. Staff use the garden for resident activities, exercise, gardening, outdoor programs, and informal dining. The garden is the completion of the overall dream to provide a quality living environment for the residents of the Helen Bader Center. All furnishings are lightweight and movable to allow for resident control and to keep loads light for rooftop safety. Cedar planters create directed pathways and alcoves for seating and are lightweight and movable for design flexibility and change. Terra cotta planters are molded plastic with a lightweight soil mixture to keep well below load limits of rooftop conditions. Awnings provide shade as well as security for the east wall to allow for free access to residents. Potting tables, storage closet, and planters are accessible for hands-on participation. The garden was made a reality through a generous gift from the family of a former resident.

Transporting pots up the elevators and through the unit draws attention.

Curtis smiles for residents observing work in progress.

Signs of use begin to appear during construction progress.

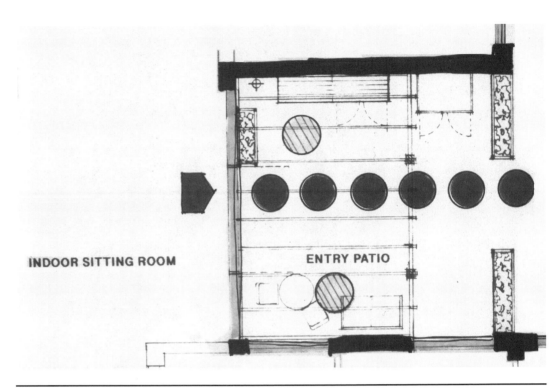

Indoor and outdoor path connection.

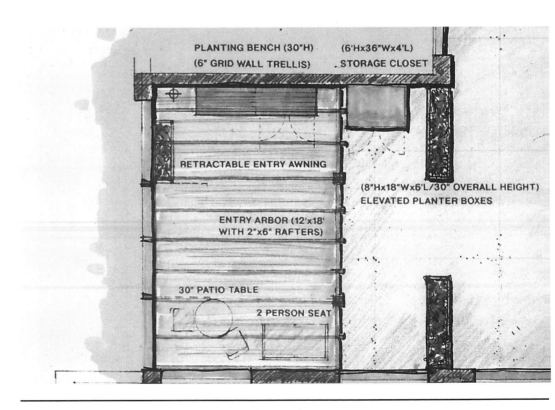

The entry patio serves as a transition and gathering place.

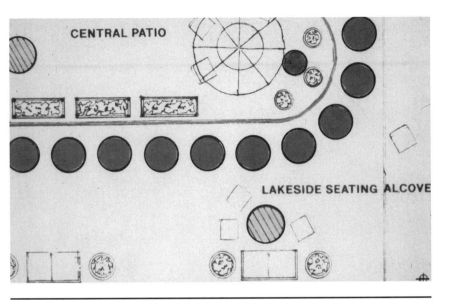

The seating area as a destination landmark.

The lakeside seating alcove creates a place to sit and enjoy the view.

The rooftop with pre-existing fixed wandering handrail before work begins.

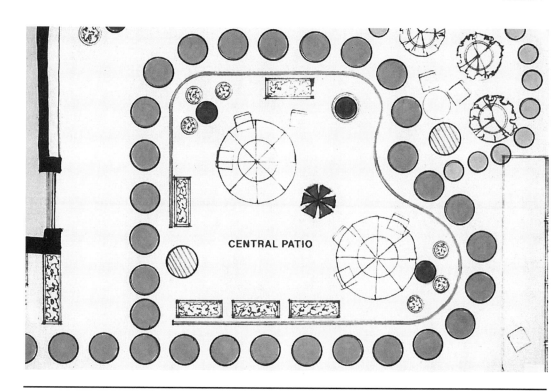

The primary walking path around railing enclosing central patio.

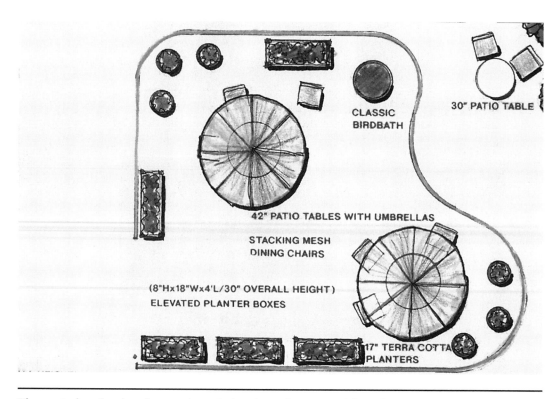

The central patio plan shows edge window box planters and furnishings.

Wood trellis panels soften the appearance of existing security fence.

Work in progress before the autumn Succoth holiday celebration.

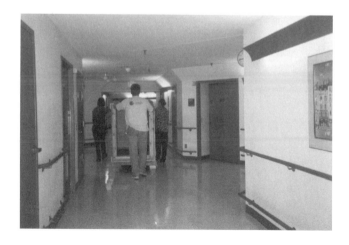

Residents begin to wonder what is going on.

Transporting the storage closet through the loading dock invites assistance.

The facilities director coordinates placement while residents observe from inside.

Positioning the raised window-box planters along inside railing edge.

Preparing the planter box liners for delivery.

Checking final details of potting tables.

Behind the scenes at the landscape nursery: preparing the soil.

A resident's tomato plants begin to ripen.

Why can't you grow summer squash in a pot?

Signs of a bountiful harvest are displayed underneath cover of the Sukkah.

Just inside the door the autumn display cues residents to changing seasons.

Rolling back the awning to prepare for the Succoth holiday (Gary Urban).

Central patio planters in place to create new inside edge (Gary Urban).

View from entry doorway after work is complete shows transformation.

3. The *Champaign County Nursing Home Alzheimer's Care Unit* is located in a university town located in central Illinois, surrounded by rural towns and fields. The Alzheimer's Care Unit is a renovated wing of the over-200-beds facility. The unit serves 14 elderly residents who have been diagnosed with Alzheimer's or a related dementia. An existing courtyard was in place with a circular walkway enclosed by a 6-foot board fence for security. A providential meeting led to the creation of a project, which became the pilot process upon which this work is based. As it was part of a design-research thesis, behavioral mapping and observations were conducted for two consecutive years.

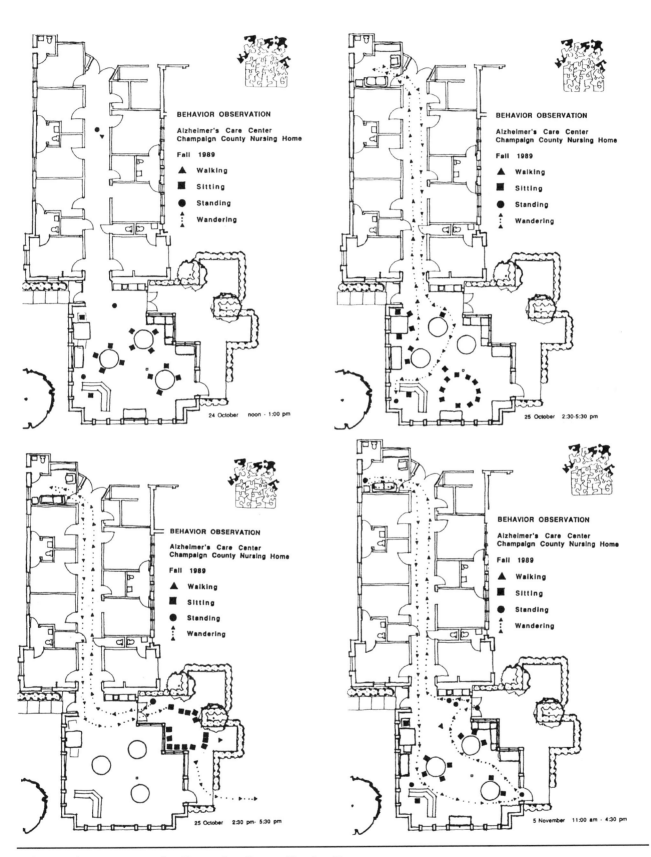

Behavior observations at the Champaign County Nursing Home.

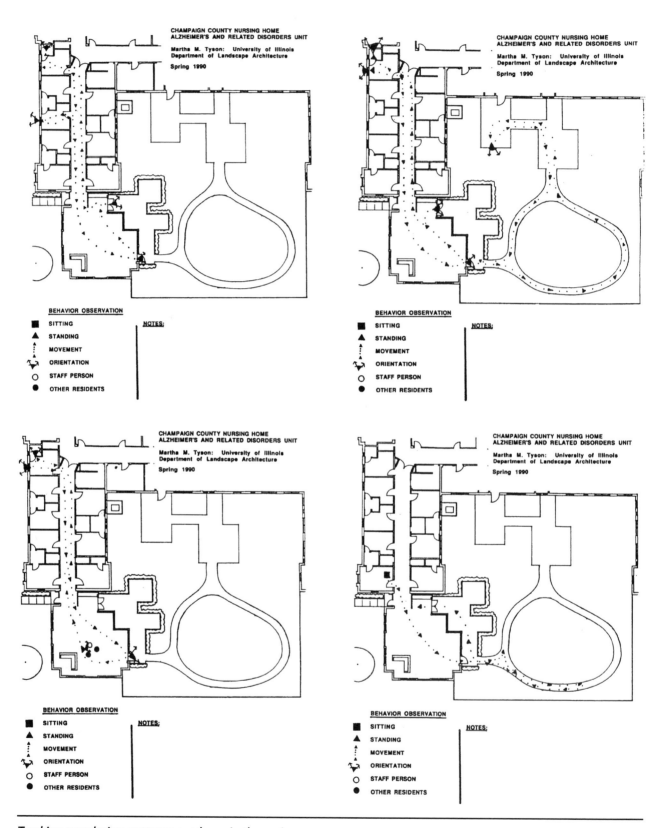

Tracking wandering patterns outdoors in the spring.

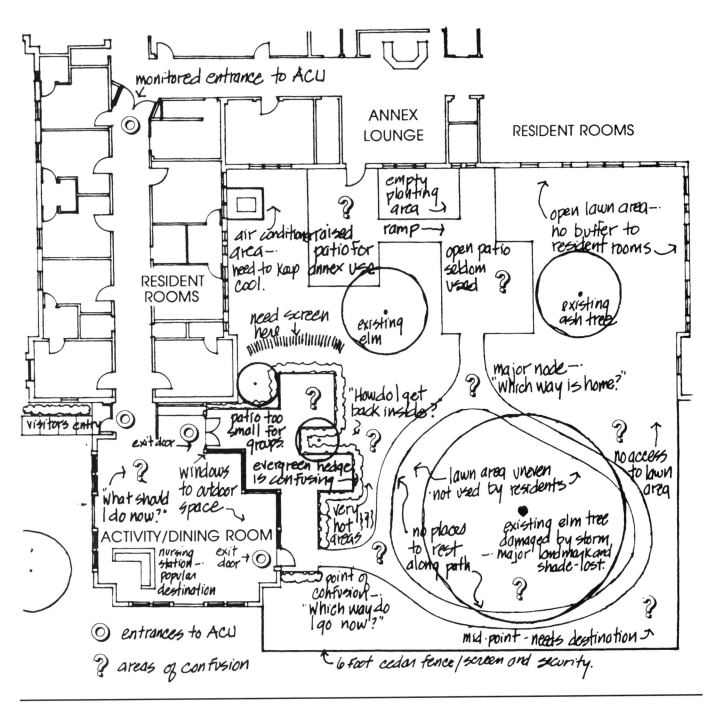

monitored entrance to ACU

ANNEX LOUNGE

RESIDENT ROOMS

RESIDENT ROOMS

empty planting area

ramp →

open lawn area-- no buffer to resident rooms →

air conditioning area-- need to keep cool.

raised patio for annex use

open patio seldom used ?

existing ash tree

?

need screen here ↓

existing elm

major node-- "which way is home?"

"How do I get back inside?"

?

no access to lawn area

"What should I do now?"

windows to outdoor space →

patio too small for groups

evergreen hedge is confusing

lawn area uneven- not used by residents →

existing elm tree damaged by storm-- major landmark and shade-lost.

very hot areas

no places to rest along path

ACTIVITY/DINING ROOM

nursing station-- popular destination

exit door →

visitors entry

exit door →

point of confusion-- "Which way do I go now"?

mid-point - needs destination →

⊚ entrances to ACU

? areas of confusion

6 foot cedar fence / screen and security.

Site and user analyses document patterns of use.

Behavior observations were conducted over a period of two years to formulate the best configuration and layout of spaces. Ordinary life of residents was observed, and interaction with the physical environment and staff or other residents was noted.

Residents and staff enjoy being outdoors on a sunny day (Champaign County Nursing Home; used with permission).

Ordinary tasks help create a family home atmosphere (Champaign County Nursing Home; used with permission).

Windows on two sides provide good indoor views of courtyard.

The design has the primary goal of encouraging people to go outside, which is accomplished through placement of plantings and landmark seating out in the yard and making access paths more direct from indoors. The existing patio was not appropriate for resident use and caused confusion and disorientation to residents who had a need to walk, as is often part of the disease progression. The patterns chosen for this project included front porch, seating alcoves, woodland garden, work bench and potting table, raised planters, grove of redbuds, lilac grove, rose garden, and upper patio.

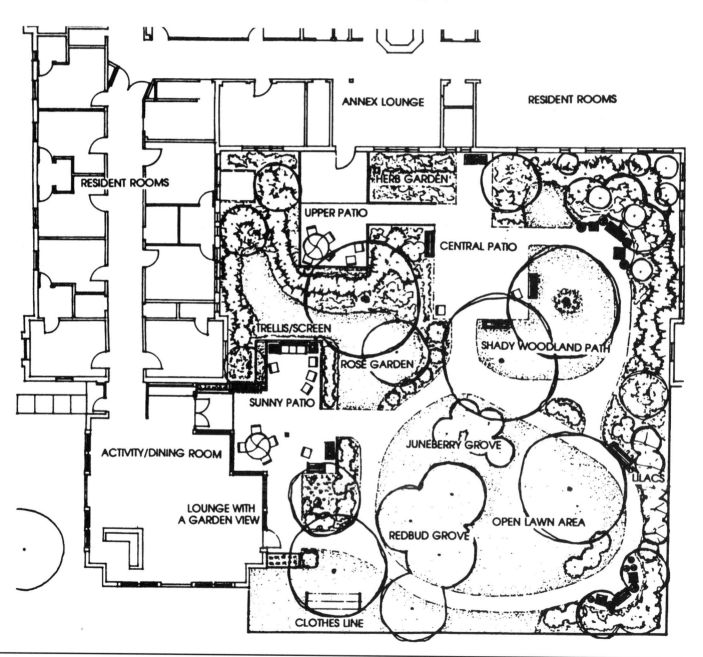

The final plan for courtyard redesign shows plantings and circulation paths.

The focus of this case study was on the *process* of involvement of students, residents, staff, family, and community members in the realization of the garden. With limited funds and a high level of enthusiasm, in the spring of 1989, the process began.

Student volunteers struggle to remove existing sod and level the ground.

Students working on preparing for planting.

Project in process begins to attract attention to the garden.

Discovery of the indoor audience of residents through the windows.

Students perform for their captive audience.

"Bernice, would you look at that little girl out there tilling the soil!"

Residents get involved in the supervision of student progress (Champaign County Nursing Home; used with permission).

Group photo opportunity at the end of the day.

Along with a few loyal classmates and friends, I went to the garden to begin removing sod, transplanting shrubs, and planting the new trees. The process continued slowly, and little by little as we progressed in our work, the residents began to watch out of the windows, come out to check the progress, and help with clean-up (sometimes weeding out the plants we just finished planting!).

Carolyn Groves and the Illinois Power Company save the day.

Students and lineman working side by side

Strategic placement of the birdbath sculpture by artist and lineman.

Administrator Joyce Ettensohn lines up the location with residents.

The grounds keeper John and Carolyn Groves survey the progress.

Residents observe progress and clean-up after workers.

The strategic progression of porch rail and flower pot, bird bath and bench.

A job well done!

A slight modification creates access from entry door to courtyard paths.

A bench as a faraway reference landmark and resting place.

Charlie observes work in progress (Champaign County Nursing Home; used with permission).

Birdbath sculpture as nearby reference landmark.

Resulting from an article about the project in the local newspaper (at the suggestion of one of the students), volunteer assistance and funding was donated by the power company and local bank, which expanded the amount of community awareness and support of the project.

Gathering marigolds (Delfina Colby, The Champaign-Urbana News-Gazette).

Staff and residents check on the new oak tree (Delfina Colby, The Champaign-Urbana News-Gazette).

University and community collaboration brings generations together (Delfina Colby, The Champaign-Urbana News-Gazette).

Students clean-up at the end of the day.

This garden had the element of life that is necessary to ensure the continued use and enjoyment of the place. Over five years later, many changes have occurred in the garden—more volunteers, donations, replacement of plants and active use by people who were not involved in the initial planting. The spirit of generosity that comes when people work together toward a common goal is somehow still working in the garden.

The design based on available research and resources of the time can be improved; however, the atmosphere created was truly successful at bringing the garden into the lives of residents, staff, and family and bringing a therapeutic benefit to all who have since taken ownership and pride in the life of the place.

Four years later the garden is still a place of family life (Robert K. O'Daniell, The Champaign-Urbana-News-Gazette).

The garden workbench.

Resident sculpture finds a home in the garden (Helen Siewers).

Cultivate Community Support

When compared to the traditional procedure followed in design and construction of landscapes, the community-supported involvement illustrated by the Champaign County Nursing Home brings a refreshing dynamism to the process. When a designer has the opportunity or time available for in-depth conversations with the people who will be using the place being designed and built, the end result will dramatically improve. Design often reflects assumed needs of potential users and takes form based on the desires of an owner or board of directors of a facility. This leads to a design that is in effect, imposed upon the people who will actually use the place. Through the structure of the process, the designer creates a solution that meets the aesthetic quality and function required for the intended purpose. The landscape designed is an interpretation of an outsider's ideas into the everyday existence of the residents or patients, staff, and visitors. When the landscape takes shape, it is installed in an efficient manner; all trees are planted, structures completed, surfaces and paths constructed until the last stone is in place. The initial excitement and interest in the process of building begins to fade at the time of "completion." In a sense the garden or landscape does not "need" anything more to sustain itself because there is not the essential sense of ownership, which is "central to the action research process" and an element for successful continuation of the design and program (Weisman, 1983, p. 399). The function and aesthetics are in keeping with someone else's "vision." Passive enjoyment and observation by one who passes by or through the space is usually the most common type of interaction, although when designed with the user's needs in mind, the place can still provide an enjoyable place for spending time. Often, the places go unused, or are not used to their maximum potential. Sometimes a lack of ownership of an outdoor area leads to a passive disinterest and decline in active social use, and eventually the physical features may begin to deteriorate from lack of maintenance. Our goal is to bring life to the process, to create places that are indeed restorative and supportive for both active and passive use. A project, however, can be renewed with life through an active program of horticultural therapy or gardening program, design modifications, or changes in activity programming. The point of this discussion is to assert that a process that includes people in "theory" and a process that invests people in "application" result in completely different places. The investment of people, of spirits and lives, brings "life" to a place. Through the investment, one tree is planted,...and then another and another. The garden is the collected "vision" of many and has evolved as a result of the participation of people who had invested in its successful completion. The garden in a sense needs the people to help it become a completed picture. While the structure is created by outside professionals, they are brought into the process by the people who are working to make it happen (Holahan, 1976). The process itself is an integral part of the healing element of the landscape and ensures the continued life and growth of the garden—it makes the place alive. (Zubee, 1991).

Cultivating community support begins with communicating the process to the key advisors and professionals involved in the project. Tapping into local resources for providing material and labor not only will provide a cost savings but will increase the public awareness of the project. This is a good time to begin thinking of sources of donations and methods of fundraising for the project, if possible. An effort to get the word out to the community via the local media is usually successful as a catalyst for bringing more people to the project. A comparison to Tom Sawyer's whitewashing the fence is appropriate to the task of turning the work into a fun process that many people "passing by" will take an interest in and seek a way to get involved. Depending on the project, the higher level of participation can take place during the planning, designing, building, or continued programming stages of the life of the garden. A community-built project is one way that requires a vested interest of key people throughout the process from early planning through the life of the garden and program. Using this process is the most dynamic as it brings entire communities together to work toward some improvement in their town, neighborhood, or facility (Hester, 1975, 1984; Leathers, 1996). A cooperative process combines the input of participants with the application of existing research and experience. The final design and installation process is a cooperative effort between professional and volunteer expertise and labor. A research-based design process has as its main goal the application of theory and research-based design guidelines that are compiled from preliminary interviews, observations, and literature review. The theory is tested through the observation of participants and use in the built environment. An evaluation is conducted to rethink the theory, make design modifications, and add to the base of environment-behavior prototypes of designs that can be modeled and used for future research study and evaluation. Finally, a garden designed with any level of participation benefits greatly from the introduction of an organized program of horticultural therapy or a well-designed activity program that includes garden-related activities in the daily schedule.

Manage Construction and Installation

With the assistance of Paul Mayhew, a collegue with extensive experience in the design-build industry, this section is intended to lay out the process of construction. Coordinating the work can be the responsibility of one or more key individuals overseeing the project. Depending on the type of project participation from volunteers who are nonprofessionals in the design and construction fields, the number of people directly involved in the project will vary. A community-built project requires the most extensive amount of planning and time; however, it usually carries a considerably lower price tag than a cooperative or research-design project. The bulk of the work is undertaken by the project coordinator who ultimately delegates tasks according to volunteer talents and skill levels in all of the needed areas. Leathers and Associates, Inc., is at the forefront of the renewed community-built movement. Robert Leathers, an architect who has committed his practice to the concept for over 20 years, builds over 125 playgrounds every year following a process that allows communities to work together to build projects that then become the personal investment of everyone who contributes. The projects generally maintain the enthusiasm of community pride long beyond the construction day and become landmarks within the community. Leathers and Associates has developed a five-step strategy for accomplishing tremendous amounts of work in a very efficient manner, with great success. A similar kind of process has been laid out for you, to involve participants in coordinated phases including communicating the process to the key advisors, coordinating site locations and defining primary user groups, organizing a design workshop with all key advisors and interested volunteers, establishing therapeutic goals for design, translating goals into design patterns, organizing the layout of the garden, composing a final plan and details for the construction, preparing the crews and project managers at an on-site meeting, laying the groundwork for construction, managing construction and large plantings, planting small shrubs, perennials and annuals, follow-up care of the garden, and organizing gardening programs or horticultural therapy sessions with patients or residents.

For the three types of projects described—community-built, cooperative, and research-design—there is a need for investment in the process by those who will ultimately use the outdoor area. It is helpful to follow the pattern of the process to assure a successful built environment that meets the needs of patients or residents, staff, and visitors, accomplishes the goals of administration, accommodates maintenance personnel, and incorporates the therapeutic criteria established for design. Other primary concerns are keeping the project within established or planned budget limits and planning for long-term maintenance.

Estimating Costs

With the final plan, an estimate can be produced based on the design. The estimate will include all site work and features in the design. Be sure all expenses are clarified at this point so there are no surprises; although the unexpected is part of the nature of working with the land and plants, most problems can be foreseen before installation. Generally the estimate includes preparation and grading, paving, planting, sodding, edging, mulching, site furnishings, irrigation, lighting, and other miscellaneous services.

The estimate should include everything needed to complete the project as agreed upon. If changes are necessary, a new estimate or partial estimate for additional work should be provided. The final estimate will vary, depending on the project size, method of installation, plant material size and quantity, paved surface areas, fencing and screening materials, and so on. A typical estimate may include demolition, removal and disposal of existing trees and undergrowth, sod, concrete, retaining walls and anything else necessary to begin grading, and landscape work.

The cost of plant material will generally include the trees, shrubs, perennials, ground covers, and annuals used in the plan as well as the labor for installation when applicable. Sodding and seeding of lawn areas are commonly estimated on a square-yard or square-foot price including installation and follow-up maintenance until a healthy stand of grass is established.

Construction work may include retaining walls, porches or decks, arbors and trellises, shade structures, awnings, planter boxes, and other built garden features. Walkways, patios, and other paved surfaces are estimated on a square-foot price that will vary considerably depending on the material used and required time for installation. Other materials and labor charges may include installation of edging, weed barrier fabric, topsoil, mulch, and fertilizer.

Fund-Raising and Public Relations

One method of defraying the costs of the garden is an organized fund-raising campaign directed at local businesses and philanthropy groups. Often with an illustrative plan of the garden and itemized report of elements and costs, it is possible to solicit donations for large portions of the garden or small elements like window boxes or flats of annual flowers. In the spirit of the participatory process, often this is an excellent way to begin promoting interest and education through the local media: television, radio, newspapers, and garden clubs. Some of the most successful projects are not those requiring a major financial investment but instead, those that have required the investment of time from dedicated professionals and enthusiastic volunteers.

Laying the Groundwork

When you have the design, there is a process of laying out or implementing the garden which continues in the line of thought of the *pattern language*. Patterns can be implemented in varied ways depending on the context, geographic and cultural-available materials, budget, and professional resources.

The principles of the patterns remain the same (Alexander et al., 1977, p. 936). The sequence of patterns follows from the original philosophy and therapeutic goals to structures and details for construction. You can watch the garden come to life as the sequences of work and patterns begin to take shape in a synchronized progression. Depending on which process design your project is best suited for—the participatory build process, cooperative, or research-design—the next phase will be conducted by key project coordinators and volunteers, or construction contractors or a research team and construction manager. This phase includes laying out the plan on the site with stakes and flags, surveyor's paint and string-lines, sometimes even people who move about the site until a desired location is selected by a group of critical eyes for the central fountain, tree, or pathway bench.

When the plan is staked out, an evaluation of the actual square-foot areas, configurations of pathways and locations of plantings and furnishings can be done. Adjustments to the plan can be made based on an evaluation of social function, location, and fit to the site as well as possible discrepancies in the plan interpretation. It is best to have all key participants review the layout and discuss any adjustments to the plan with the construction manager and project designer. Take care to invite the groundskeeper and maintenance staff to review the plans on site, as this will bring up issues that may be prevented by slightly altering the design layout.

Design has a twofold purpose: function and form or artistic expression. In this process the form is derived from the function, or "structure follows social spaces." "No building ever feels right to the people in it unless the physical spaces (defined by columns, walls, and ceilings) are congruent with the social spaces (defined by activities and human groups)" (Alexander et al., 1977, p. 941).

According to the *Timeless Way of Building*, there are four principles to follow in this way of thought and path to construction of a living garden. First, the spaces must physically respond to the psychological and social needs of those who will be using the garden. If this elemental philosophy of design is overlooked, you may forfeit the end result of a place that is calming and relaxing. Test the design by studying the function and fit of the actual layout according to the original design goals and plan. The second principle is to give the people who use the space some understanding of its structure and how it has been composed. An example of this is to use materials and construction methods that are familiar (while keeping in mind the physical features necessary to assure safety). Selection of construction materials, furnishing styles, and plant varieties depend on the geographical, cultural, and architectural context of the project. The third principle is to assure that the social space is supported by its surroundings and that the design and materials are congruent with the building edge and uses and enclosing elements. The fourth principle is to create some sense of definition of the perimeters or corners of the space (Alexander et al.,1977, p. 944). The overall goal is to allow social spaces to dictate the form, working in harmony with the architectural form and building layout.

Installation

Not all projects begin with necessary resource dollars. If you have a limited budget but have a lot of landscaping to do and can not afford it all at once, you have a few options. One option may be to phase in your project a little at a time, setting priorities in what you need done first. In fact, a project that is always somewhat "in process" is a benefit to the concept of a living garden. "An environment which is ordered in precise and final detail may inhibit new patterns of activity. What we seek is not a final but an open-ended order, capable of continuous further development" (Lynch, 1960, p. 6).

An overall site plan will allow the project to be phased in over time. This has a twofold benefit: first, to save on the labor and installation cost by doing some of the work in-house or with volunteer help, and second, to involve people in the process of bringing the garden to life. To organize the work under the direction of a designer and alongside or with a professional installation crew requires both coordination and education. The long-range benefits of continued use and ownership are important to keep in mind. This phase of the project is often the most memorable and sets the tone of community spirit and cooperation. As mentioned earlier, the more participatory the process, the more time and coordination necessary to keep the project moving along on schedule.

In some circumstances, it may be more effective to have a professional crew do the heavier construction portion of work to completion and work alongside the volunteer consortium under the direction of a landscape architect or construction manager for the remaining planting and light construction.

Depending on the scope of the project and methods of installation, the project can take anywhere from one to two days to two to three months or years to complete. Large projects may require periodic construction meetings with allied professionals working on the project (e.g., engineers, architects, and contractors) to coordinate work and schedules and to address problems in the field. Regardless of the size or scale of the project, communication is the key to a successful installation. Frequent site visits by the key project advisors and the designer during the process is a valuable way to keep the project moving along and reduces the number of problems and design changes later. Although it may seem costly at first to spend this preliminary amount of time throughout the process, in the end it will help to assure that the quality of the work meets client expectations and needs as well as prevents overlooking concerns or problems that occur along the way (Zick, 1994).

Construction

The installation process varies from project to project but generally follows a logical pattern. The first step involves the location of utilities, including telephone, electric, water, sewer, gas, cable, and other underground or above-ground lines through the site. Next is the site demolition work, which includes removal of vegetation, existing patios, walls, and constructed elements. Site grading and landform construction includes leveling and smoothing areas for walkways, planting, or lawns as well as creating desired contours or mounded areas according to the design.

It is important to locate utilities before each phase of the work begins, to prevent possible accidents or damage to existing lines. Keep careful watch, because paint markings on the ground or flags identifying locations of utility lines often will be removed during construction work, leaving the door open for trouble. Installation of new hard scape elements will be the first phase of actual construction work. Patios, decks, pools, walkways, and retaining walls are included in this phase of work. Site lighting involves the coordination of electrical work with site work. Fixed pathway lighting and light poles will usually require the professional assistance of the lighting designer or a manufacturer's representative.

The final stage involves the landscape work. Planting areas are generally defined first, then fine grading and top soiling is completed before any planting work begins. Irrigation systems involve crossing over planting beds and lawn areas to connect to the main water source; therefore, planting of trees, shrubs, perennials, and ground covers can be begun after staking locations according to the plan. A later phase of the installation is usually seeding or sodding, and annual plantings.

Following the construction work, planting, and clean-up, an inventory of the workmanship and condition of plant material is conducted by the designer or construction manager with each contractor to make necessary changes and repairs. At this time the project coordinator or designer may wish to review the process with participating contractors and key project advisors to discuss any ideas or issues concerning the project, construction, or future programming and care.

Evaluating the Progress

When the work is complete and the dust is settled down, it is time to ask the questions: Does the completed project meet the original goals? How did the budget compare with actual costs? Is the site able to be maintained as intended? The nature of landscape design and the creation of gardens is that the landscape is always changing. Plants grow, mature, and change with the seasons. Weather conditions are unpredictable; wood structures, pathways, and furnishings weather with years of use and exposure to the elements. All of these things are what give the garden its unique character and sense of place; however, unlike places indoors, they require more frequent maintenance and observation to ensure the safety of residents, which is always the primary concern.

Developing a Maintenance Program

In order to reduce the possibility of unsafe conditions, it is critical to be aware of settling that may occur on walkways or patios over time, thresholds at doorways, shaded areas that may cause slippery conditions on paved surfaces, transitions between lawn areas and pavement, splitting of wood construction or benches, and connecting points on tables, chairs, or awnings. If these conditions are identified and repaired immediately, unnecessary accidents may be prevented. The goal is to provide a safe, enjoyable outdoor place for patients or residents, staff, and family, and to improve the quality of life.

Maintaining the garden area is an important part of the project. It is helpful early in the process to decide how you are going to maintain the new landscape. Maintenance issues include what is necessary to keep the plantings alive, paths clean, and lawns mowed—that is, the overall general maintenance program. Develop a maintenance program along with the final design and make provisions in the budget for continued follow-up care such as irrigation, snow removal, and mowing. Allow places for equipment and vehicle access through fences for repairs or emergency situations. It may be your intention that the residents take care of some plants on the site. This may require raising the planters so that residents are able to pick weeds and water plants or using a variety of container gardens, window boxes, and vertical planting systems.

Introduce Horticultural Therapy

As the element of continuity between design and programming, the introduction of horticultural therapy is one way to ensure continued use and participation in the garden project. The benefits of a gardening program are primarily for the physical well-being of participants, secondly for the increase in active use and social life of the outdoor places, and thirdly for the image of a refined flower garden. "In horticultural therapy, plants are grown specifically for the restorative and rehabilitative effects they might have on a person growing them. The primary objective is to heal the patient; producing plants and flowers is a secondary benefit" (Lewis, 1979, 1990).

Horticultural therapy as an academic discipline is relatively young; however, the practice of horticultural therapy in the United States dates back to the late 1700s. Its history is rooted in agriculture and health care for mentally ill patients of the Friends Asylum, now Friends Hospital, located in Philadelphia. The profession is allied with both occupational therapy and horticulture with growing involvement in environmental psychology and design. As a point of reference, horticultural therapy programs established in the United States (i.e., the Chicago Botanic Garden and the Rusk Institute in New York) are often used as models for both national and international programs in the process of being developed. Other programs that are well established are in the United Kingdom— for example, Horticultural Therapy Garden, Battersea Park in London, is a community-based garden that operates through charitable funding and the work of volunteers including people who experience mental health problems or sensory or physical disabilities (Jones, 1992).

According to research conducted through Horticultural Therapy, an organization dedicated to the education and furthering of programming of horticultural therapy in the United Kingdom, benefits of gardening activities are physical, social and emotional. For example, to improve dexterity in finger and arm strength, a therapist may engage a client in an activity of repotting a seedling or watering houseplants using a lightweight watering can. To improve mobility, clients may be encouraged to walk along paths through the garden. To help clients cope with difficult emotional situations, growing plants that produce flowers or fruit like tomatoes or annual flowers can help people look forward to the harvest or bloom time. To assist clients in developing social skills, programs can form gardening clubs or shared activities that may bring people together in a friendly setting. Designing gardens to support this kind of activity requires an understanding of how a therapist would most benefit from a design.

According to Rosemary Hagedorn, an occupational therapist who reflected on how the landscape design can facilitate therapeutic activities; if a garden is intended for the use of a garden program, the surroundings should reflect a "back garden" where "one might expect to pull weeds and pick flowers." The desired behavioral interaction that is necessary for the therapist to work most successfully with patients will be encouraged if the place looks and functions like a "working garden" (Hagedorn, 1990, p. 21). The integration of therapeutic measures into the designed environment and programming introduces an active dimension of the healing process.

Programs that incorporate horticultural activities enable residents to grow flowers, vegetables, or herbs for their use in the kitchen or for crafts. "The power of gardening to heal and help us grow has been recognized since the beginning of civilization. Used therapeutically, nature and gardening have helped restore people to health through both the restful and quiet viewing of lovely gardens and the sunlight, fresh air, and moderate exercise offered by outdoor gardens" (Moore, 1989,

p. 3). Simple gardening can provide a familiar activity that can be accomplished with clear and simple directions by a staff person. These people can benefit from an environment rich in sensory and physical elements that provides cues for orientation to time, place, and purpose. "A richly planted garden area can provide material for reality orientation. The therapist is provided with many opportunities for verbal cues such as 'Look at the beautiful yellow daffodils,' 'What a lovely spring day,' and for the use of actual objects in activities such as picking the fruit and then being able to eat it" (Hagedorn, 1990, p. 21).

When planning and designing outdoor spaces for people who suffer from some medical condition that impairs cognition or physical abilities, it is critical to realize that often it is the little things that can make a big difference. By designing a place that accommodates familiar daily activities, it is possible to offer residents or patients and staff the opportunity of working together to continue with normal outdoor tasks like watering a window box or potting a geranium. People with sensory or cognitive impairment may benefit greatly from highly sensory interaction with plants. The familiar smell and sight of lilacs or roses, the taste of a fresh tomato from the vine, the feel of smooth leaves from an oak tree, or soil warmed from the sun are sensory experiences that one can experience only in the garden (Healy, 1991).

This anecdote from a book entitled *Grandma's Garden* illustrates the unspoken quality of working the soil.

"Carefully she straightened, one hand on her knee, the other on her hip, and grimaced as her bones creaked and complained about assuming a new position. The sun beat down unmercifully. She removed her hat and wiped her wet brow with a lace handkerchief stuck in the bosom of her blouse. Her hands, gnarled and weathered, were evidence of years of gardening in the sun. The wrinkles lining her face spoke of age and wisdom. Slowly she hobbled to a nearby bench and sighed heavily as she dropped her body onto it. She put her hat back on her head and looked around. The grimace became a smile. Her eyes twinkled with joy as she surveyed her garden. She turned to me. 'It's a good garden, Laura. The good Lord and I have done a lot of work here'" (Martin, 1990, p. 5).

Evaluate

CHAPTER 4

The Process Comes Full Circle

Evaluation brings the process full circle. This phase is the beginning of a rethinking and redesigning path, bridging gaps between research and design. Arriving at the final phase of our journey of investigating, designing, and building a place where people can experience the restorative qualities of nature, we pause for a moment and think about where we have been and what path to follow from here. Our journey began with the exploration of the essence of a healing landscape, the thoughtful selection of symbols and patterns of design, the careful composition of patterns, and the process of investing people in the building of their garden place. Designers undertaking the design of a healing environment often seek concepts that symbolize or reflect some aspect of the healing process. When evaluating the therapeutic value of the experience for people using the garden, although the underlying symbolism may be the inspiration behind the design, it is the observed use of the garden that is most often the indicator of therapeutic benefit.

As introduced in Chap. 2, we interpret the world around us through our understanding of symbols. "The study of thinking, learning and memory is based on the idea that thinking relies on the interpretation of symbols, which provide us with a kind of shorthand, both saving time and space and providing a logic and organization which our brains can handle" (Brookhart et al., 1992, p. 8). Symbols, depending on their universal appeal, can vary greatly in the way they are interpreted and understood by people using the garden. Referring to the comparison of the composition of poetry in Chap. 3, "Although the poet may pin down the meaning of a symbol to something fairly definite and precise, more often the symbol is so general in its meaning that it can suggest a great

Exploring the essence of a landscape.

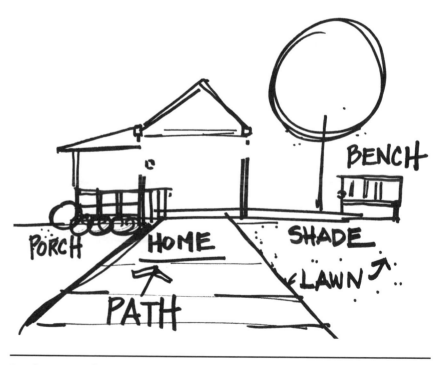

Landscape symbols.

Symbol translated into place (Daniel Sjordal).

variety of meanings (Perrine, 1988, p. 586). Each design concept is, in a similar way, a composition of patterns and images chosen for creating places that get to the heart of what makes a garden that promotes or supports healing. The precise metaphorical meaning attached to the garden is most effective when it translates into universal design patterns that take shape into an outdoor place that is comfortable, restful, supports ordinary activities of the therapeutic program, and is accessible for everyday use.

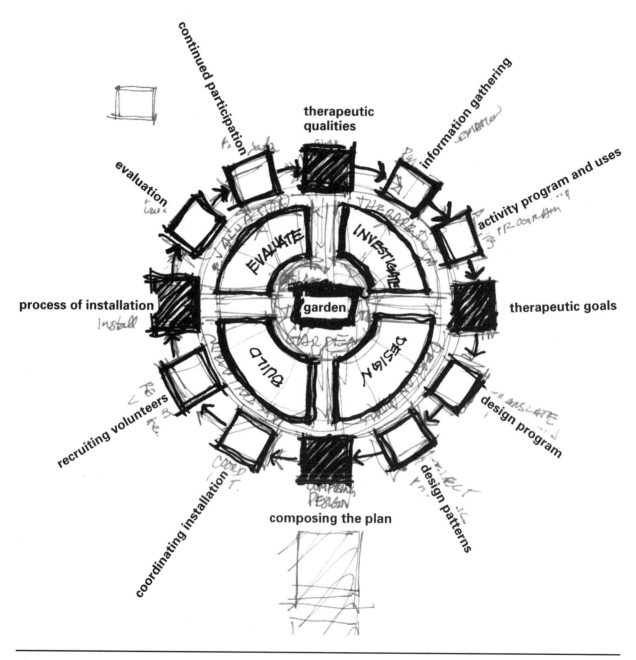

The process comes full circle.

Daily walk (Daniel Sjordal).

Observations of Ordinary Life

Stories of how people spend time outdoors or relate to the garden areas can begin to define what features may make one place more conducive to healing than others. I offer the following personal anecdotes as examples of an adventurous but rather unorthodox method of seeking person-place associations in the ordinary events of daily life. While walking through a public garden in Germany, I happened upon an elderly woman and her daughter seated on a bench along the promenade. I stopped for a time to sketch a bit of the scenery, and a conversation arose. We exchanged stories of gardens, and the older woman told of their daily walks from her residence at the far end of the park, to see the new flowers and to stroll to the tea house for afternoon tea. It was not until well into this animated conversation that I realized that I was speaking in English, she in German, and her daughter somewhere in between. The entire conversation took place in some form of universal language, although I did have the sketchbook and could use it in referring to the plants and trees as we walked along. I accepted an invitation to visit the residence in the afternoon, and the event continued with coffee and cookies with her other daughter, who arrived with a basket of cookies for her mother, in the outdoor dining area at her home. This encounter would prove to change the course of my search for symbolic meaning in the everyday life of the garden.

On another wandering, I came upon a most delightful cottage in western England overflowing with bright pink, blue, and purple flowers. I decided to take a closer look. After passing through the gate, I found a group of elderly residents tending to their plants and enjoying the morning sun. After greeting them and visiting for a while, I noticed that the garden was a living example of the features I knew to be conducive to healing and well-being for elderly people. Ten years of inquiry, and I found the answer in the simplicity of this little garden! Residents had planted containers along the patio edge with flowers and vegetables (including corn and tomatoes), and bird feeders and simple birdbaths were located at strategic places in the garden. The sense of enclosure and continuity with the indoors was precisely what I would imagine it should be. Presently, I was invited back for cream tea and scones in the afternoon. We visited in the cozy kitchen overlooking the garden, and I learned that the home was renovated to accommodate elderly people with cognitive impairments and that the garden (which played a major role in the program) was created for and by the residents. I began to wonder what it was about this particular garden that was so comfortable and inviting.

The ordinary life of the garden.

A view from the lane.

The search for the fountain.

While traveling the narrow streets of a Spanish village, I encountered a very old woman who appeared to be lost and in need of assistance. It was very hot in the late afternoon sun. In my limited Spanish, I asked if she needed anything or someone to take her home. "La fuente! La fuente!" was all I could gather from her rapid and extended explanation of her seemingly serious state of distress. She began to walk, and motioned me to follow. My "feeble" yet speedy companion and I walked along the narrow streets, up and down the steep hills. She spoke in unceasing and rapid Spanish, showing me the trees and plants along the way. She talked, and we walked, and the sun beat down. Beginning to be a little concerned after more than an hour of our lesson in the native flora, I tried again to ask her where she lived and where we might be going. "La fuente, vale…vale…la fuente!" was all that I could understand. After rounding a corner, we arrived at a beautiful promenade of trees, a shady walkway with benches for resting. She continued on, talking and walking with more enthusiasm than ever, until she arrived. "A fountain!?" I said out loud to myself. She motioned for me to follow her. Reaching with both hands into the water, she splashed cool water on her face and hands and smiled. Her eyes sparkled with joy. "La fuente…" I thought as I sat down on the edge of the pool. Then I smiled at my discovery, my new-found friend, and the wonderful simplicity of it all.

Informal observations and anecdotes provide a real-life perspective of direct benefits of contact with the natural world. However, when considering a method of evaluation, we need to decide what we want to accomplish with the evaluation. It may be sufficient just to know that

La fuente.

people are enjoying and using the garden, and further research is not necessary. However, if the process of inquiry becomes more defined, it may be necessary to use structured methods to gather information about the influence of the built garden on participants' or residents' behavior. An objective data collection method is also more likely to provide for the application to other similar situations.

William H. Whyte, known for his ability and propensity as a "professional observer," is recognized by planners and architects as a master of *people watching*. His work evolved into a way to systematically wait and watch…and watch and wait. "You will begin to see patterns develop," he says. "Begin by making small changes,…and you will be able to have a tremendous effect on the environment and people's perception of it." Although directed to urban New York street life, Whyte's straightforward approach tells us that what we often overlook as ordinary and not worthy of research is in fact what is at the heart of the life of places. Whyte explains the value of keen observation: "Planners get so busy doing things that they don't check out their findings on the street. Many technical questions can be answered by a few days of research" (Dillon, 1996, pp. 74–75). In Whyte's often-quoted study of urban plazas, *City and the Social Life of Small Urban Spaces*, there are some simple truths. For example: People sit where there are places to sit, and the street is a river of life through the city, and what attracts people in the city is other people (Whyte, 1980). Beyond observations and systematic mapping of behaviors, a postoccupancy evaluation is a structured method of collecting information about the use of built places.

Postoccupancy Evaluation

Postoccupancy evaluation involves taking a look at the built project in terms of how it is actually being used. More specifically, a postoccupancy evaluation is "a systematic evaluation of a designed and occupied setting from the perspective of those who use it" (Cooper Marcus and Francis, 1997, p. 345).

Conducting a *postoccupancy evaluation* (POE) is a form of research directly related to developing a program of use as discussed in Chap. 1. The general purpose of conducting a POE "concentrates on the needs of building occupants and their response to their environment, providing insight into past design decisions and, in effect, establishes a pool of experience by which designers and owners alike can benefit" (Marcheso Moreno, 1989). The purpose of the evaluation from a research and design perspective is twofold: to check the reliability and validity of the research design by identifying features that are successful and unsuccessful, and to recommend revisions to the particular project assessed and considerations for future similar projects. Studies that involve the evaluation of special needs user groups involve a more specific set of criteria set to measure the therapeutic outcomes of design (Cooper Marcus and Barnes, 1995; Zimring, 1995). Other uses for a postoccupancy evaluation are to obtain feedback on existing sites, gather information for future designs, increase the cost-effectiveness of projects, to identify user perceptions, and improve development decisions (Marcheso Moreno, 1989). Allied design disciplines such as architecture and urban planning have a history of success in working with evaluative tools (Preiser, Visher, and White, 1990). An increase in the common use of some form of evaluation of built projects among landscape architects will result only in improvements in future designs and studies (Cooper Marcus and Francis, 1997).

In practice, a postoccupancy evaluation has the potential to play an increasingly important role in the construction of and renovation of existing garden areas. In general practice, information gathered from a post-construction evaluation gives the owner and architect the opportunity to make on-site changes to either meet the original contract specifications or improve the design as it has been constructed. This type of evaluation is important to ensure that the construction work is acceptable and according to the design; however, evaluation of how the design functions for the people who use it is often overlooked. In reference to this reality, Clare Cooper Marcus and Carolyn Francis address the issue from the point of view of traditional professional process: "After the completion of the building or outdoor setting, it is typical for the design team to move on to another job; it is very rare for them or their clients to return to the site after a year or two of use to conduct a systematic, objective evaluation" (Cooper Marcus and Francis, 1997, p. 356).

Design can benefit from ongoing evaluation that opens a dialog for improvement and increased use. Furthermore, the publication of information from these evaluations (both successful and unsuccessful features of built gardens), especially for specific use—healing gardens—will benefit the greater design community. In an elemental form, postoccupancy evaluations are recorded observations of people in the outdoor space. I spent some time watching and recording people in a garden designed using some of the principles described earlier. "It's a wonderful place to stop and think." I was impressed with the profound simplicity of these words from a resident of the Hearthstone Alzheimer Care residence, where I was observing the active use of the garden. We were sitting together on the "front porch," which was intended to be a place for informal visits and a place to look out into the yard. That is all she said to me as we sat that afternoon, she in her glider and I on an old wicker chair. A place to stop and think. I observed other residents walking or visiting with family. A few came out for an afternoon snack, and one man slept a while on a bench in the far corner of the garden.

At the Champaign County Nursing Home, one of the most successful outcomes of the garden was that, as the process of installation progressed, the number of people invested or involved in the garden

METHODS   — OUTDOOR AREA

☐ E-B CHECKLIST

☐ FOCUSED INTERVIEWS → Residents
    Staff
    Family → Their use (with residents)
              opinion/perception
              impact
              Evaluation

☐ QUESTIONNAIRE — STAFF

Assoc mens
Interactive Eval
  · behav. what/don't
  · friendly /don't
  · pleasant
  · feelings.

- associated
  Memories/recollection
1. Interaction what/don't why?
2. USES how how often, who opinion
3. serve needs?

1. GM Successful features
2.   Uses

independence
affection
relaxation   sleep patterns
                    social links

People → people
People → environment

interaction Environment People

need for
privacy

health
of blush

☐ BEHAVIOR OBSERVATION STUDIES

    ☐ Behavior Log (5-10 minutes x/day
        · outdoor
        · indoor - in adjacent room

    indoors ☐ Behavior Mapping =13 zones every __ minute
    outdoors

    ☐ Behavior Tracking SR 13 plant bed
        R
        R S (RRS)
        RR

    Where people are HOW MANY

    How movement / time spent

☐ RECORDS ANALYSIS R S F
    ☑ - Accidents How many
    - Elopement
    - Behavioral change ±

    # Negative Response falls Elopement

☐ SPACE-PLAN measure Total SF
                        Zone SF
                        Distances

    Adequate space for activity
    Proportions

☐ POLICY Procedures
    · Formal written
    · Unwritten rules (from interview)
                      admin. form
                      Prog. ? w

    What is allowed personalization use times

☐ Physical Conditions.

    ☐ damage. wear & tear
    ☐ replacements /plants

    Do Plantings need replacement or
    moved _ Furnishings ?
    painting?

☐ Photo graphic Documentation.

Evaluation tool: E-B checklist (J. Zeisel/Tyson).

increased. One example is an elderly resident who had been a farmer all his life. He showed a marked difference in his behavior and attention to the outdoors after we began working in the garden. It was inevitable that when we would arrive, Charlie would already be outside surveying the yard and cleaning up sticks and leaves that had fallen on the lawn or paths. It was not until I was giving a presentation to a seminar class of architecture students at the University of Minnesota that I discovered that in each of my slides describing the process, there was Charlie—picking up sticks, observing the workers, or giving instructions. Years beyond the days of our initial installations, until the end of his stay on the unit, Charlie spent hours in the yard, everyday.

Another resident who was not very involved in the social life of the unit and who appeared to have well-advanced Alzheimer's disease, decided to go outdoors one summer afternoon. She took scissors outside, to the alarm of attending staff who carefully observed as she calmly walked out to the rose garden. She carefully selected a rose, reached into the rose bush, removed two sets of leaves, snapped off the thorns near her cutting area to prevent getting poked, and cut the rose. She proudly carried the rose indoors, and placed it into a vase on the table. She had been a rosarian, and she was just engaging in what was a very familiar activity for her. This kind of event is telling of the significance of the universal familiarity of a garden. At least for these few people, we can assert that there are definite positive therapeutic outcomes. These evaluations are the basis for more rigorous postoccupancy work and behavioral research studies. The growing number of studies in environment-behavior research invite us to apply existing information to our projects and adapt the research to fit our particular needs to evaluate how people are using the places we build (Cooper Marcus and Francis, 1997; Hester and Francis, 1990; Sommer and Sommer, 1986; Zeisel, 1984; Zube and Moore, 1987, 1991).

Continual revision and successive evaluation of design, built environments, and social happenings will be accomplished only through an open and ongoing evaluative process. In assessing the process as it has been laid out in the previous chapters, we are led to a constant rediscovery of the complex relationships between person, place, and interaction. When a garden is designed to maximize optimum functioning in patients with cognitive or physical disabilities, it is important to define some measurable outcomes; for example, range of motion may be increased by the activity of raking leaves. Therefore, we ask, does our designed garden facilitate residents' freedom and ability to rake leaves? If yes, how well have we accomplished this, and can we make improvements. If no, how can we adapt the design or program to support this particular therapeutic outcome. Is it an issue of management, programming, or design?

The evolution of the process shows the constant change and evaluation necessary for the ongoing life and improvement to best meet the individual needs of patients or residents who will be impacted by the

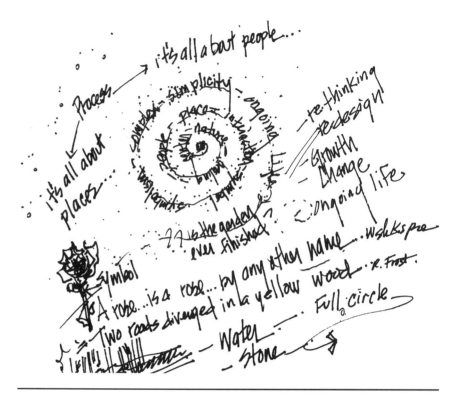

Person-place relationships: "It's all about people."

Preparing for the leaves (Daniel Sjordal).

healing environments we set out to create. When we explore each phase of the process as it relates to person, place, and interaction, we become increasingly aware of the integral synergy affected by the process itself (Holahan, 1976). In reviewing the phase of investigation, we may ask ourselves: How well have we addressed the personal needs of individuals who are actually using the garden area? Were we correct in our assumptions or investigation of who would be the primary users of the place? Are people interested and involved in the ongoing life of the garden? In reference to the place: How appropriate is the site for the type of garden use? Does the specific microclimate prove to be conducive to maximum use and comfort? Is the surrounding context (indoor and off-site use) in keeping with the spirit and use of the garden area?

Investigating people-place interaction (M. Inouye/S. Levine).

Reviewing design for people-place fit (M. Inouye/S. Levine).

Postconstruction review of build phase (M. Inouye/S. Levine).

Evaluation brings the process full circle (M. Inouye/S. Levine).

Specific to the interaction of people in the garden, we may ask: How accessible, both visually and physically, is the garden to patients or residents who would most benefit from some contact with the outdoor area? Do windows and doors allow for choice of involvement from a distance or active use? Does the garden support appropriate activities and current use patterns?

In the design phase, we can look at how well the design responds to individuals' needs. For example, if a person has an impaired gait pattern, does the design of paths and destinations provide the necessary surface requirements and visual cues to encourage independent use? Concerning the actual physical structure, are the features constructed soundly so as to prevent hazardous situations as much as possible? Are there any hidden corners or barriers that need to be addressed? Does the design reflect the original intent? Referring to interaction with the garden, were we successful at creating a place that encourages personal ownership and spontaneous use? Are plantings, benches, and garden features that were intended for direct interaction being used or enjoyed as originally intended?

In the build phase, we are concerned about how well the built garden functions as a catalyst for involvement beyond the actual construction phase. Are staff, residents, or family members open to suggest change and alternation to best meet the needs of patients? Is the place successful at providing appropriate amounts of space for planned or unplanned activities that can be observed? Was the process successful at coordinating the installation and volunteer effort to bring the garden to reality? How successful was the actual installation process in accomplishing goals and providing an opportunity for open involvement and conversation between varied groups involved—for example, medical personnel, gardeners, residents, staff, family members, design professionals, and contractors?

Apply Design Improvements

Following a postoccupancy evaluation, a report should be made of successful and unsuccessful features of both the social and physical functioning of the design. Evaluations conducted within a short time after construction will often allow for immediate change-orders and design revisions. Evaluations conducted after the site has been in use for some time will usually require more detailed documentation and analysis. The same methods of environment-behavior research used for collecting data for design are often used to collect data to use in analyzing existing designs in use. The application of results from postoccupancy evaluations is effective from a practical use view and financial savings on future projects. If possible, conduct an evaluation before and during the actual con-

Have we accomplished what we set out to do? (M. Inouye/S. Levine).

struction. Often this will require change-orders in design and construction; however, it is more efficient to change a drawing than to take out a sidewalk and reroute circulation after construction is completed. This requires the designer or project manager to acquire some basic research skills and have a clear understanding of the final purpose of design.

The goal of evaluating the process is to determine whether we have created a garden that realizes our original intent. Acceptance and involvement from the administration to front-line staff, is essential in the process of preparing the groundwork for the ongoing success of the garden. Through the chain of events involved in the creation of one of these healing gardens, the garden becomes not only a beautiful place to spend time but a real catalyst for changing social patterns for the better (Holahan, 1976). In comparing this kind of participatory process with the traditional design process, the focus is on the *individual* as opposed to the place (Francis 1979). *Action research* implies that there is a change in the normal course of activites and that some outside element is a catalyst for change.

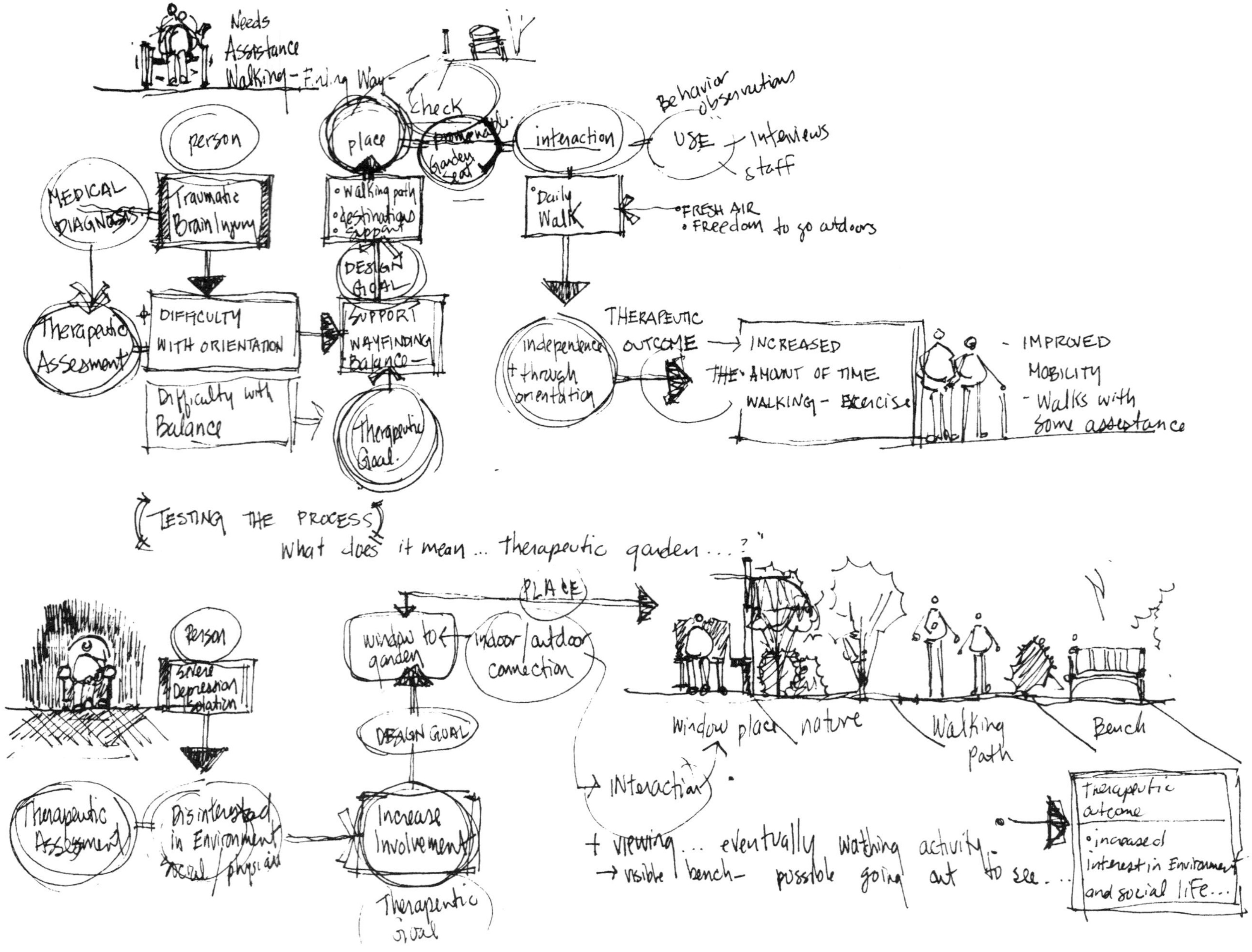

Needs Assistance Walking — Finding Way

Person
Traumatic Brain Injury
MEDICAL DIAGNOSIS
Therapeutic Assessment

DIFFICULTY WITH ORIENTATION
Difficulty with Balance

behavior observation
USE interviews staff
Interaction
Check...

Place
• Walking path
• destination support
DESIGN goal
SUPPORT WAYFINDING BALANCE
Therapeutic Goal

Daily Walk
• FRESH AIR
• FREEDOM to go outdoors

THERAPEUTIC OUTCOME → INCREASED THE AMOUNT OF TIME WALKING — EXERCISE
Independence through orientation

— IMPROVED MOBILITY
— Walks with some assistance

(TESTING THE PROCESS) What does it mean ... therapeutic garden ... ?

PLACE
Window for indoor/outdoor garden
Indoor/outdoor connection
DESIGN GOAL

Window place nature
Walking Path
Bench

→ INTERACTION
→ VIEWING ... eventually walking activity
→ visible bench — possible going out to see ...

• therapeutic outcome
• increased interest in environment and social life ...

Person
Severe Depression
Therapeutic Assessment
Disinterested in Environment social physical

Increase Involvement
Therapeutic goal

Testing the process.

A description of the action research process is similar to that which we have used to describe the process evolution: "A big spiral of steps,...each composed of a circle of planning, action and fact finding about the result of the action" (Lewin, 1946). Kurt Lewin, a pioneer in the discovery of the benefits of action-based design, considers the three elements—action, research, and training—to be like the three sides of a triangle that cannot be separated. Lewin asserts that the process is seeking the solution of social problems and is continual—repeated and repeated. Training researchers (and designers) to translate research into built projects requires a cooperative relationship between research and practice. In order to accomplish this kind of association, training is essential to develop a way to clearly communicate the information to both design and nondesign professionals. John Zeisel, in *Inquiry by Design* (1984), describes design development as a "spiral metaphor"

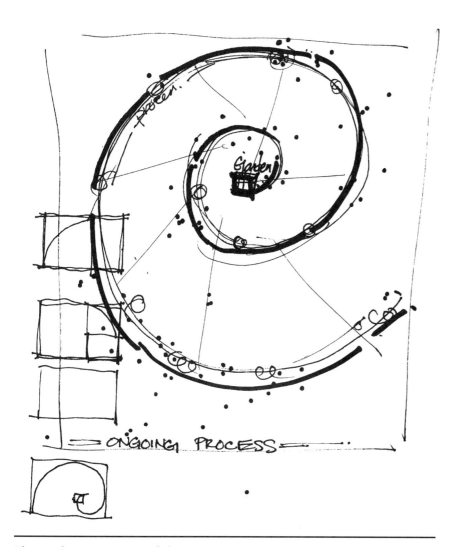

The garden as an agent of change.

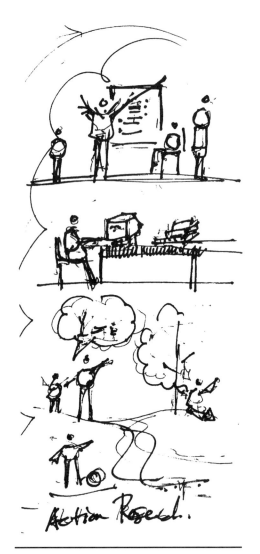

Action research and design.

that reflects the pattern of thinking that designers go through when solving a design problem. *Backtracking* through the process to revise or alter previous design decisions and to repeat previous design activities with a shifted focus, together with the simultaneous movement of backtracking, repetition, and linking the cycles of imaging, presenting, and testing brings the designer closer to an application to a built solution (Zeisel, 1981, pp. 14–18).

Advances in both design and research depend on the availability of research information, education, and application in built projects. According to one research study in environment-behavior and design, there are three models for bridging the gap between research and application—information transfer, education, and action research. Information transfer includes "research dissemination and translation" (i.e., design guidelines, codes, and regulations) and "research consumption" (i.e., policy development, programming, postoccupancy evaluation, and built form and design exploration).

Education involves the transfer of information and theory to designers and potential users of built environments. The education incorporates both design disciplines (i.e., professional and academic education) and nondesign user education (i.e., trade journals and community-based research). The final model *action research,* is the direct application of theory to built environments. This may include collaboration between design and research professionals on a particular project, a more direct form of developing theory while actively working on a solution or intervention to create some environmental or social change (Schneekloth, 1987).

Although the boundaries between research and design are often clouded in these dual-purpose projects and require refinement, the

Educating.

Facilitating.

insight and new knowledge generated are assets to the growing discipline of environment-behavior research and practice. As mentioned in the section on investigation, the development of a program of use is an essential part of the process, however, it is often misunderstood and as a result, it is difficult to facilitate its utilization (Weisman, 1983). The process of environmental programming is designed to develop a "detailed set of goals and requirements [program] for a specific planning or design project."

Participatory design and planning focus on bringing people together to take part in the process (Hester, 1984; Leathers, 1996). When the projects are linked to ongoing research, they usually have several objectives: successful design interventions (solutions), generation of new knowledge, and the transfer of knowledge (Schneekloth, 1987).

Procedures for facilitating the practical application of research may best be used in a real-life context, using an action research approach to solving problems. Action research is defined by its cyclical nature with the intent of investigating, developing theory, applying theory to design, and evaluating the built design (Weisman, 1983; Susman and Evered, 1978; Wisner et al., 1991). The designer or researcher becomes an integral part of the process—a participant as well as facilitator. The ability to communicate or translate from the language of all participants is essen-

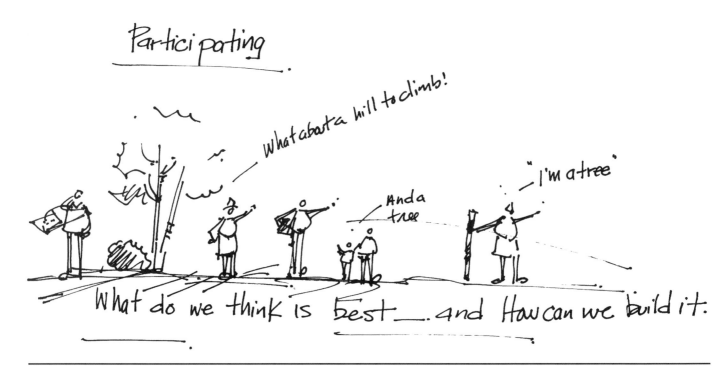

Participating.

tial to the success of the project. In effect, the action researcher acts to get to the heart of what we want to accomplish to how the built place will project the therapeutic character we set out to create.

The designer who plays the role of *action researcher* holds a critical place in the progressive integration of these principles into the everyday design process (Zube and Moore, 1991). Formal evaluative research projects and investigative instruments that build on the foundations of environment-behavior theory and practice offer objective and measurable outcomes from which to draw conclusions for design adaptations and directives. Within the coming decades, we will begin to see an emerging new generation of work in this area and movement toward bridging gaps between the world of research and the world of practice.

The evaluation of a built garden would benefit from a critical review based on a few simple inquiries:

1. Can we create tools available to practicing design professionals to use for evaluating built projects that help identify positive "therapeutic outcomes" to residents or patients, staff, and visitors?

2. When conducting a postoccupancy evaluation, are designers and researchers able to discern which elements are successful at accomplishing the intended therapeutic outcomes, and which are not?

3. Are we able to use the evaluation tools to provide practical recommendations for design revision and future project programming?

As these inquiries take form, complex overlays of person-place interactions need to be simplified and brought back into the overall process.

The complex-simplicity described in the introduction can be described through the use of the golden ratio in the form of the nautilus or the golden spiral. The form of the spiral is based on simple geometric forms and a repeated pattern of squares and rectangles. The geometric planes and forms used to construct the spiral become increasingly more complex mathematically, while at the same time, the image created becomes visually more simple and understandable (Garland, 1987). Closely related to the golden ratio is a sequence of numbers 0, 1, 2, 3, 5, 8, 13, 21,…, known as the *Fibonacci series,* which creates patterns that are found in the natural world of flowers, leaves, branching patterns, and seashells. This series of numbers, the *golden sequence,* ties together the golden section and the Fibonacci series of numbers (University of Surrey, 1997). A discussion of the mathematical theory behind these concepts is beyond the scope of this book, but it does have direct links to art, architecture, and design (Obernolte, 1983). We can look, however, at the simplicity of form and pattern of the golden spiral as it relates to the process coming full circle, initiating change, and repeating the pattern of the process over and over again, with infinite boundaries. The process of action research initiates change. Evaluation recommends adaptations. Building gives form to ideas. Design generates solutions. Investigation defines person-place associations. The form of the spiral seems to fit the concept of continual evaluation—thinking, redesigning, rebuilding, reevaluating, again and again, moving toward an outdoor environment that is fully supported and produces positive therapeutic outcomes.

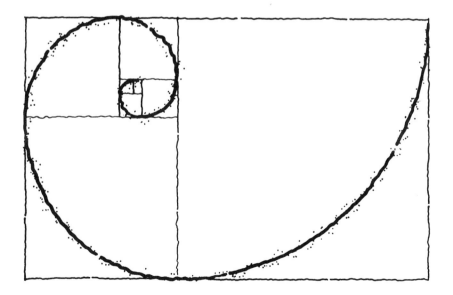

The golden spiral (M. Inouye/S. Levine).

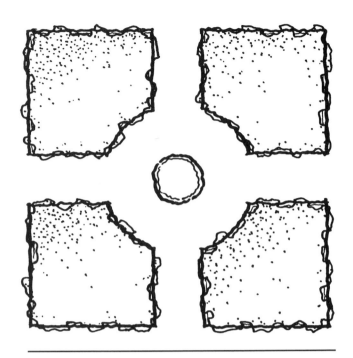

The completed garden as a symbol of process (M. Inouye/S. Levine).

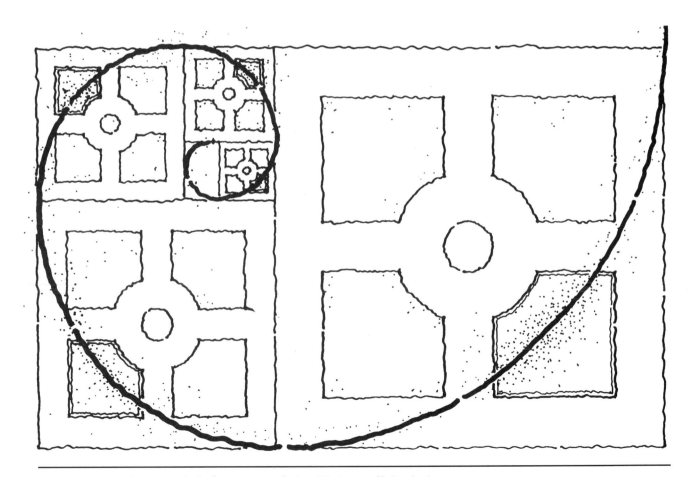

The golden spiral as a symbol of process evolution (M. Inouye/S. Levine).

Recommend Future Research Paths

After extensive study and research on healing garden design, David Kamp (Loeb Fellow at Harvard University, 1995–1996) presents some thought-provoking questions to consider when undertaking the design of a healing garden. What are the principal motivations behind building these gardens? How can they be successfully integrated into the changing health care system? "Will the struggle between science and commerce also include compassion? Will our values allow nature to contribute to and expand our concepts of health, healing, and well-being? Or, will the garden become a tool for cosmetic imagery? Marketing? Ultimately asking the question: Is there a place for nature in twenty-first-century health care?" (Kamp, 1996, p. 5).

In the light of working toward a greater body of knowledge, both scientific and less traditional behavioral research studies are necessary to explore, evaluate, and quantify the therapeutic outcomes of interaction with purpose-designed landscapes. Multidisciplinary avenues of research, conducted with a common goal, will naturally lead to advances in the professions allied in the effort to build a stronger foundation for the work of future endeavors. Complementary medicine (holistic healing) is growing in acceptance as are alternative forms of therapy that include aroma therapy and use of natural remedies to help in the healing process.

Complementary or integrative treatments and therapies constitute more than a trend. People want these options and will take the initiative to seek out physicians and health care professionals who follow the holistic way of thought on healing. A 1993 study quoted in a *Life Magazine* issue featuring "healing revolution" showed that one in three Americans chose to use alternative therapies, to the extent of an estimated $14 billion (Howe-Colt, 1996).

In harmony with traditional Western medicine, the combined approach offers the technological advances in conjunction with appropriate herbal remedies and healing practices; you would not treat a person who suffers from a traumatic head injury and other complications with flower essences, just as you would not treat a common cold with major surgery. *Integrative medicine* offers people the option to take an active role in their own healing process (Pera, 1997).

Anne Pera, a registered nurse and healing arts practitioner describes the garden adjacent to Marin General Hospital's oncology radiation waiting room as a "way to soften the blow." The whole wall is glass so the garden is "right there," where patients can see and go outside. "It makes the place come alive." The garden contains plants from which the chemotherapeutic drugs are derived. The garden allows patients to become involved in their healing process.

Although proven by centuries of use, much of the research is descriptive, qualitative in nature, and lacking in the hard-science data required for gaining recognition among those in the medical and administrative professions. Empirical research-design collaboration produces projects with apparent far-reaching benefits to the participating and future users as well as design and research professionals, however, in the scientific arena of quantitative research, the results are often considered less significant than studies conducted using more traditional research models (Weisman, 1983).

Groundbreaking quantitative research shows a significant improvement in the rate of recovery of patients who are exposed to views of nature as opposed to views of a solid brick wall in a postsurgery hospital setting (Ulrich et al., 1984) and that the same holds true for a significant decrease in stress-related physiological symptoms in a later study (Hartig et al., 1991). These efforts are beginning to bridge another gap between the environmental psychology and behavioral research disciplines and hard-science medical disciplines.

Upon review of existing literature on therapeutic and healing gardens, Dr. Joanne Westphal, a licensed physician and associate professor in the Michigan State University Landscape Architecture Program, set up a framework of research issues that may be addressed in the assessment of gardens designed with the intent of providing healing qualities. First, identify which groups of patients are most appropriate to study using cause-and-effect measurement methods. The second issue addresses design intervention as a means of "preventing, reducing or altering the outcomes of particular diseases." The third issue, upon which many future projects will ultimately depend for application, is how the concept of healing gardens will fit into the present American health care delivery system (Westphal, 1997). This open forum in both scientific research and exploratory studies, which, when compared and combined, will build the base of research knowledge and practical design directives for the next generation of landscapes and healing gardens. A pilot study examined the role that a view of nature might play in the workday environment of ICU nurses. The research took place at units at two Midwestern medical centers. One ICU had a lounge with large windows overlooking mature trees and buildings; the other lounge was windowless. The nurses were asked to do a task and then rate themselves on an affect grid that measured arousal and mood while they were giving patient care in the morning. After their noon break in their lounges, they were asked to repeat the task and self-rating. The group with the window had significantly reduced stress levels and made fewer errors on the task than the group with the windowless lounge. The puzzling but encouraging finding is that the group with the window performed more accurately than the other group despite the fact that the work environment was more stressful (Ovitt, 1996). These types of studies are increasingly important in the introduction of the therapeutic value of design within the medical and health care community. Other studies conducted by cross-disciplined professionals (i.e., design and medical training and experience, environmental psychology and design) are beginning to open the dialog of healing gardens to professionals outside of the design disciplines (Gerlach et al., in process; Healy, 1997). No doubt there will be a continued line of study, research, and practice that will build upon the existing foundations, for example (Carey, 1986; Carpman et al., 1986; Cooper Marcus and Barnes, 1995; Hartig et al., 1990; Healy, 1997; Kaplan and Kaplan, 1990; Lewis, 1995; Paine and Francis, 1991; Relf, 1992; Stoneham and Thoday, 1996; Ulrich, 1984, 1992). "Insight into practice which both creates new knowledge and theory, and which engages in environmental and social change, is an important task facing our field. Our research and our practice will be richer for such inquiry" (Schneekloth, 1987).

Future directions in research will depend directly on the sharing of knowledge and open dialog among professionals within allied design fields and the associated health care and environmental psychology disciplines with whom collaborative efforts will occur. To confirm and restate the belief that the preceding work is not intended to be a prescriptive method of planning, designing and building healing landscapes: My purpose in translating thoughts on small pieces of paper collected over the past 15 years is to lay out a path for continued work and describe a way of thinking, thus opening new paths in the search for meaning in ordinary life, in nature, in human behavior, in design, and in the art of composing living tapestries of plants and people for the purpose of healing.

"What is essential is invisible to the eye."
—Saint-Exupéry, 1943, p. 70

APPENDIX

Garden Use Questionnaire

Windows

1.   Are there windows that residents are able to look out without making an extra effort, such as opening blinds, standing, or straining?

❏ yes   ❏ no

2.   How often do you notice residents looking out the windows during the day?

❏ very often   ❏ often   ❏ sometimes   ❏ rarely   ❏ never

3.   Please describe what you feel they are looking at most often.

_____
_____
_____
_____
_____
_____
_____

4.   How often do you notice that seasonal changes affect resident's mood?

❏ very often   ❏ often   ❏ sometimes   ❏ rarely   ❏ never

5.   In what ways are residents affected by seasonal changes?

_____
_____
_____
_____
_____
_____
_____

Resident Behavior

6.   How often do you need to intervene with residents who tend to wander or pace?

❑ very often   ❑ often   ❑ sometimes   ❑ rarely   ❑ never

7.   Have you observed that residents who wander seem to follow a pattern?

❑ yes   ❑ no   ❑ not sure

8.   If yes, please briefly describe/draw the general pattern below. Please note with an X apparent landmarks or specific destinations.

9. In the last year, have any residents wandered away from the home?

    ❏ yes   ❏ no   ❏ not sure

10. How likely are these possible reasons why someone may have been able to wander away?

	Very likely				Not likely
Unsecured outdoor space	❏	❏	❏	❏	❏
Apparent agitation	❏	❏	❏	❏	❏
Expressed need to go somewhere	❏	❏	❏	❏	❏
Followed someone outdoors	❏	❏	❏	❏	❏
Faulty monitoring system	❏	❏	❏	❏	❏
Pattern of behavior	❏	❏	❏	❏	❏

    Other reasons: _____

    _____

11. When responding to resident's restless behavior, how often do you use these calming techniques?

	Very often				Never
Soothing discussion	❏	❏	❏	❏	❏
Walking with resident indoors	❏	❏	❏	❏	❏
Walking with resident outdoors	❏	❏	❏	❏	❏
Suggesting a change of activity	❏	❏	❏	❏	❏
Giving them time alone	❏	❏	❏	❏	❏
Physical restraint	❏	❏	❏	❏	❏
Medication	❏	❏	❏	❏	❏

    Other techniques: _____

    _____

12.   How successful do you feel your existing outdoor space is for the following?

	Very successful				Not successful
Staff surveillance from inside	❏	❏	❏	❏	❏
Security for wandering residents	❏	❏	❏	❏	❏
Observing nature/birds	❏	❏	❏	❏	❏
Small group gathering	❏	❏	❏	❏	❏
Allowing residents to wander safely	❏	❏	❏	❏	❏
Easy access to the outdoors	❏	❏	❏	❏	❏
Visiting with family/friends	❏	❏	❏	❏	❏
Organized group activity	❏	❏	❏	❏	❏
Encouraging reality orientation	❏	❏	❏	❏	❏
Helping residents feel independent	❏	❏	❏	❏	❏
Privacy for quiet visiting	❏	❏	❏	❏	❏

13.   How often is your outdoor space used for the following activities (in good weather)?

	Often				Never
Family visits	❏	❏	❏	❏	❏
Planned group activities	❏	❏	❏	❏	❏
Celebrations/picnics	❏	❏	❏	❏	❏
Staff breaks	❏	❏	❏	❏	❏
Quiet visiting with residents	❏	❏	❏	❏	❏

Other activities: _____

_____

14. If residents do not use the outdoor space, how likely are these possible reasons?

	Very likely				Not likely
The area is not enclosed	❏	❏	❏	❏	❏
The area is exposed to sun, wind, etc.	❏	❏	❏	❏	❏
The area is not attractive to residents	❏	❏	❏	❏	❏
There is nothing to do outside	❏	❏	❏	❏	❏
Residents are not allowed outside alone	❏	❏	❏	❏	❏
Doors are not accessible to residents	❏	❏	❏	❏	❏
Entrances are locked	❏	❏	❏	❏	❏
Area is perceived as unsafe by staff	❏	❏	❏	❏	❏
Residents feel insecure when outdoors	❏	❏	❏	❏	❏

Other reasons: _____

_____

15. When residents use the outdoor space, how often do you observe them engaged in the following activities?

	Very often				Never
Sitting in the shade	❏	❏	❏	❏	❏
Sitting in the sun	❏	❏	❏	❏	❏
Observing nature/birds	❏	❏	❏	❏	❏
Watching activities	❏	❏	❏	❏	❏
Wandering	❏	❏	❏	❏	❏
Doing garden-related work	❏	❏	❏	❏	❏
Walking with others	❏	❏	❏	❏	❏
Walking alone	❏	❏	❏	❏	❏
Visiting with others	❏	❏	❏	❏	❏
Organized activity	❏	❏	❏	❏	❏

Other observations: _____

_____

16.   How capable do you feel most of your residents would be for the following activities?

	Very capable				Not capable
Repotting plants	❏	❏	❏	❏	❏
Planting seedlings	❏	❏	❏	❏	❏
Walking outdoors	❏	❏	❏	❏	❏
Bird/animal watching	❏	❏	❏	❏	❏
Light gardening tasks	❏	❏	❏	❏	❏
Watching gardening activities	❏	❏	❏	❏	❏
Light yard work/raking leaves	❏	❏	❏	❏	❏
Watering the lawn/flowers	❏	❏	❏	❏	❏
Hanging laundry on a clothes line	❏	❏	❏	❏	❏
Filling a bird feeder or bath	❏	❏	❏	❏	❏
Mowing the lawn (push mower)	❏	❏	❏	❏	❏

17.   How much does your existing outdoor space encourage the following responses from residents?

	Very much				Not at all
Increase in general awareness	❏	❏	❏	❏	❏
Maintaining daily life skills	❏	❏	❏	❏	❏
Reestablishing links to familiar events	❏	❏	❏	❏	❏
Support abilities	❏	❏	❏	❏	❏
Compensation for losses	❏	❏	❏	❏	❏
Respite from indoor stress	❏	❏	❏	❏	❏
Freedom to go outdoors	❏	❏	❏	❏	❏
Sense of ownership	❏	❏	❏	❏	❏
Independent use	❏	❏	❏	❏	❏
Security for family	❏	❏	❏	❏	❏
Staff respite	❏	❏	❏	❏	❏
Encouragement of normal social roles	❏	❏	❏	❏	❏
Physical exercise	❏	❏	❏	❏	❏

Other: _____

Designing the Outdoor Space

Your task now is to help to create an outdoor space for your residents, staff and family. Please rank the following features on a scale of 1-10, 1 being the *most important* and 10 the *least important* for your residents.

_____ Patio for group gathering
_____ Open lawn area for games
_____ Quiet conversation areas
_____ Pathway with several loops
_____ Strolling garden
_____ Garden visible from indoors
_____ Screened porch
_____ Seating areas in sunshine
_____ Seating areas in shade
_____ Indoor sun room with plants
_____ Area screened from noise around the site
_____ Others: _____
_____
_____

18.   Safety and security

_____ Total area visible by staff from indoors
_____ Security fence (no view out)
_____ Security fence (views out)
_____ Nontoxic plants
_____ Level pathways
_____ Monitored entrances
_____ Soft residential lighting for night use
_____ Pathways that loop back to beginning
_____ Others: _____
_____
_____

19. Trees, flowers, and gardening

_____ Shade trees/fruit trees
_____ Ornamental flowering trees
_____ Flowering shrubs
_____ Flowers
_____ Fragrant plants
_____ Garden plots
_____ Container gardens
_____ Work area/potting shed
_____ Tool storage
_____ Small greenhouse
_____ Others: _____
_____
_____

20. Furnishings/site features

_____ Benches with backs and arms
_____ Lightweight movable seating
_____ Clothesline for hanging laundry
_____ Bird feeder
_____ Bird bath
_____ Fountain/pond
_____ Yard art/decorations
_____ Porch/yard swing
_____ Play equipment for children
_____ Others: _____
_____
_____

Now please list the three most important items in each category.

21.   Places: _____
           _____
           _____

22.   Safety: _____
           _____
           _____

23.   Trees: _____
           _____
           _____

24.   Features: _____
           _____
           _____

Thank you for your time and effort in preparing this questionnaire. The information will be used to develop design programs for future outdoor spaces and renovations to existing gardens.

BIBLIOGRAPHY

Alexander, C. 1979. *The Timeless Way of Building.* New York: Oxford University Press.

Alexander, C., et al. 1977. *A Pattern Language.* New York: Oxford University Press.

Alliance for the Mentally Ill (AMI) of Wisconsin. 1996. *Family and Consumer Resource Guide,* 3d ed. Madison, Wis.

American Horticultural Therapy Association (AHTA). 1988. Newsletter. Gaithersburg, Md.

American Psychiatric Association (APA). 1994. *Diagnostic and Statistical Manual of Mental Disorders,* 4th ed. (DSM-IV). Washington, D.C.

Anderson, T. 1990. Provision for the Elderly Mentally Ill. *Landscape Design,* no. 198 (April), pp. 23–24.

Anthony, K. A., 1990. Seminar in E-B Studies, University of Illinois, School of Architecture.

Appleton, J. 1984. Prospects and Refuges Re-visited. *Landscape Journal,* vol. 3, no. 2.

Appleton, J. 1990. *Prospects and Refuges.* University of Illinois at Urbana-Champaign, School of Architecture.

Appleton, J. 1996. *The Experience of Landscape,* rev. ed. New York: Wiley & Sons.

Bailey, R., C. H. Hardin Branch, and C. W. Taylor (eds.). 1961. Architectural, Psychology and Psychiatry: An Exploratory International Research Conference, February 24–25, 1961, at the University of Utah, Salt Lake City, with the National Institutes of Health.

Berrall, J. 1966. *The Garden: History.* New York: Viking.

Betrabet, G. 1997. From History into the Future: The Shaping of the Landscape into Places for Restoration. Ph.D. dissertation, University of Wisconsin, Milwaukee School of Architecture.

Bite, I., and M. J. Lovering. 1984. Design Opens Doors for the Elderly. *Landscape Architecture,* November/December, pp. 79–81.

Bite, I., and M. J. Lovering. 1985. Design for the Elderly. *Landscape Architectural Review,* vol. 4, no. 3, pp. 9–14.

Brookhart, S., et. al. 1992. *Exploring the Brain.* Washington, D.C.: National Institute for Brain Research.

Butterfield, D. W. 1982. Outdoor Spaces Surrounding Group Homes for the Developmentally Disabled Adult. M.A. thesis, University of Illinois, Department of Landscape Architecture, Urbana, Ill.

Calkins, M. 1988. *Design for Dementia: Planning Environments for the Elderly and Confused.* Owings Mills, Md.: Williams & Wilkins.

Campbell, D. T., and J. C. Stanley. 1963. Experimental and Quasi-Experimental Designs for Research on Teaching. In N. L. Gage (ed.), *Handbook of Research on Teaching.* Chicago: Rand McNally.

Carey, D. A. 1986. *Hospice Inpatient Environments: Compendium and Guidelines.* New York: Van Nostrand Reinhold.

Carpman, J. R., M. A. Grant, and D. A. Simmons. 1986. *Design That Cares: Planning Health Facilities for Patients and Visitors.* American Hospital Publishing, a Subsidiary of the American Hospital Association.

Carstens, D. Y. 1985. *Site Planning and Design for the Elderly: Issues, Guidelines and Alternatives.* New York: Van Nostrand Reinhold.

Carstens, D. Y. 1990. Housing and Outdoor Spaces for the Elderly. In Cooper Marcus and C. Francis (eds.), *People Places*. New York: Van Nostrand Reinhold, ch. 5.

Chen, A. W. 1985. Try a Change of View. *The Toastmaster*, November, pp. 19–21.

Clemence, R. 1988. *The Meanings of Place*. Independent study, University of Minnesota, Minn.

Cohen, U., and J. Weisman. 1991. *Holding on to Home*. Baltimore, Md.: Johns Hopkins University Press.

Conley, T. 1997. Personal interview concerning Robert Frost M.A. thesis, Cleveland, Ohio.

Coons, D. 1988. Wandering. *The American Journal of Alzheimer's Care and Related Disorders Research*, vol. 3, no. 1 (January/February), pp. 31–36.

Cooper Marcus, C. 1978. Remembrance of Landscapes Past. *Landscape*, vol. 22, no. 3, pp. 35–43.

Cooper Marcus, C., and M. Barnes. 1995. *Gardens in Healthcare Facilities: Uses, Therapeutic Benefits, and Design Recommendations*. Martinez, Calif.: Center for Health Design.

Cooper Marcus, C., and C. Francis (eds.). 1990. *People Places*. New York: Van Nostrand Reinhold.

Cooper Marcus, C., and C. Francis (eds.). 1997. *People Places*, 2d ed. New York: Van Nostrand, Reinhold.

Dannenmaer, M. 1995. Healing Gardens. *Landscape Architecture*, vol. 85, no. 1, pp. 56–58.

De Long, A. J. 1970. The Micro-Spatial Structure of the Older Person: Some Implications of Planning the Social and Spatial Environment. In L. Pastalan and D. Carson (eds.), *Spatial Behavior of Older People*. Ann Arbor: University of Michigan Press, pp. 68–86.

Dillon, D. 1996. The Sage of the City. *Preservation Magazine*, September/October, pp. 71–75.

Dowling, J. 1995. *Keeping Busy*. Johns Hopkins, University Press, Baltimore, Md.

Escrivá, J. 1988. *Furrow*. New Rochelle, N.Y.: Scepter.

Francis, M. 1979. *Participatory Planning and Neighborhood Control*, Center for Human Environments, City University of New York.

Frost, R. 1916. *Complete Poems of Robert Frost*. New York: Holt, Rinehart and Winston.

Garland, T. 1987. *Fascinating Fibonaccis: Mystery and Magic in Numbers*. Palo Alto, Calif. D. Seymour Publications.

Gerlach, N., Kaufman, D., and Warner, S. B. n.d. In process. Yale University Press.

Goltsman, S., et al. 1992. *The Accessibility Checklist: An Evaluation System for Buildings and Outdoor Settings*. Berkeley, Calif.: MIG Communications.

Greene, E. 1990. *The Legend of the Christmas Rose*. Retold from the Original by Selma Lagerlof (1907). New York: Holiday House.

Hagedorn, R. 1990. Occupational Therapy and Environmental Consciousness. *Landscape Design*, no. 189, April, pp. 21–22.

Hardman, M. L., et al. 1993. *Human Exceptionality: Society, School and Family*, 4th ed. Needham Heights, Mass.: Simon and Schuster.

Hartig, T., M. Mang, and G. Evans. 1991. Restorative Effects of Natural Environment Experiences. *Environment and Behavior*, vol. 23, pp. 3–26.

Healy, V. 1991. Personal interview concerning the use of plantings in hospice and health care settings. University of Illinois at Urbana-Champaign. April 26.

Healy, V. 1997. Personal interview concerning the therapeutic value of lilacs and fragrance in health care facilities. March 28.

Heim, K. 1985. Creativity Takes Sides. *The Toastmaster*, November/December, pp. 16–18.

Hester, R. T. 1975. *Neighborhood Space*. New York: Dowden, Hutchinson, and Ross.

Hester, R. T. 1984. *Planning Neighborhood Space with People*, 2d ed. New York: Van Nostrand Reinhold.

Hester, R. T., and M. Francis (eds.) 1990. *The Meanings of Gardens: Idea, Place and Action*. Cambridge, Mass.: MIT Press.

Holahan, C. J. 1976. Environmental Change in a Psychiatric Setting: A Social Systems Analysis. *Human Relations*, vol. 29, no. 2, pp. 153–167.

Howe-Colt, G. 1996. The Healing Revolution, *Life Magazine*, September, pp. 34–50.

Jensen, J. (1939) 1990. *Siftings: Ralph Fletcher Seymour*, Chicago, Ill.: Johns Hopkins University Press.

Jones, R. 1992. Commotion at Battersea. *Growth Point (Newsletter of Horticulture Therapy, U.K.)*, no. 191 (summer).

Kamp, D. 1996. Healing Environments: Restorative Gardens. *Loeb Fellowship Forum Magazine*, Harvard Graduate School of Design, Spring/Summer 1996, pp. 4–6.

Kaplan, R. 1973, Some Psychological Benefits of Gardening, *Environment and Behavior*, vol. 5, no. 2, pp. 145–161.

Kaplan, R., and S. Kaplan. 1990. Restorative Experience: The Healing Power of Nearby Nature. In R. Hester and M. Francis (eds.), *The Meanings of Gardens: Idea, Place and Action.* Cambridge, Mass.: MIT Press, pp. 238–243.

Kaplan, R., and S. Kaplan. 1996. *The Experience of Nature: A Psychological Perspective,* 2d ed. New York: Cambridge University Press.

Kidder, L. H., and C. M. Judd with E. R. Smith. 1986. *Research Methods in Social Relations.* New York: Holt, Rinehart and Winston.

King, R. 1979. *The Quest for Paradise.* New York: Mayflower Books.

Landsberg, S. 1995. *The Medieval Garden.* New York: Thames and Hudson. *Landscape Design.* 1990. Editorial. No. 198, p. 2.

Leathers, R., and Associates. 1996. *Step by Step: Innovative Strategies for Community-Built Structures and Other One-of-a-Kind Architectural Projects.* Ithaca, N.Y.: Leathers and Associates.

Levin, B. E. 1990. Spatial Cognition in Parkinson's Disease. *Alzheimer Disease and Associated Disorders: An International Journal,* vol. 4, no. 3 (fall), pp. 161–170.

Lewin, K. 1946. Action Research and Minority Problems. *Journal of Social Issues,* nos. 1–2, pp. 34–36.

Lewis, C. A. 1973. *People-Plant Interaction: A New Horticultural Perspective.* American Horticulturist, vol. 52, no. 2, pp. 18–24.

Lewis, C. A. 1976. *The Evolution of Horticultural Therapy in the United States.* National Council for Therapy and Rehabilitation through Horticulture, Lecture and Publication series, vol. 2, no. 5 (October), Mount Vernon, Va.

Lewis, C. A. 1979. Healing in the Urban Environment: A Person/Plant Perspective. *Journal of the American Planning Association,* no. 45, pp. 330–338.

Lewis, C. A. 1990. Gardening as Healing Process. In R. Hester and M. Francis (eds.), *The Meanings of Gardens: Idea, Place and Action.* Cambridge, Mass.: MIT Press, pp. 244–251.

Lewis, C. A. 1995. *Green Nature, Human Nature.* Urbana, Ill.: University of Illinois Press.

Lindenmuth, G. F., and B. Moose. 1990. Improving Cognitive Abilities of Elderly Alzheimer's Patients with Intense Exercise Therapy. *American Journal of Alzheimer's Care and Related Disorders and Research,* vol. 5, no. 1 (January/February), pp. 31–33.

Liss, L. 1986. Letter to the editor. *The American Journal of Alzheimer's Care,* vol. 1, no. 4 (fall), p. 5.

Lovering, M. J. 1990. Alzheimer's Disease and Outdoor Space: Issues in Environmental Design. *American Journal of Alzheimer's Care and Related Disorders and Research,* May/June, pp. 33–40.

Lynch, K. 1960. *The Image of the City.* Cambridge, Mass.: MIT Press.

Mc Arthur, M. G. 1988. Exercise as Therapy for the Alzheimer's Patient and Care Giver: Aggressive Action in the Face of an Aggressive Disease. *American Journal of Alzheimer's Care and Related Disorders and Research,* vol. 3, no. 6 (November/December), pp. 36–39.

Mace, N. L. 1993. Observations of Dementia Specific Care around the World. *American Journal of Alzheimer's Care and Related Disorders and Research,* vol. 8, no. 3 (May/June), pp. 1–8.

Mainardi-Peron, E., et al. 1990. Effects of Familiarity in Recalling Interiors and External Places. *Journal of Environmental Psychology,* vol. 10, pp. 255–271.

Marcheso Moreno, E. 1989. The Many Uses of Postoccupancy Evaluation. *Architecture,* April, pp. 119–121.

Marshall, L. L. 1983. *Action by Design: Facilitating Design Decisions into the 21st Century.* Washington, D.C.: American Society of Landscape Architects.

Martin, L. 1990. *Grandma's Garden: A Celebration of Old-Fashioned Gardening.* Marietta, Ga.: Longstreet Press.

Mayhew, P. D. 1997. Selected Professional Practice Issues. Stacey, Minn: Unpublished.

Mooney, P., and P. L. Nicell. 1992. The Importance of Exterior Environment for Alzheimer Residents: Effective Care and Risk Management. *Healthcare Management Forum,* vol. 5, no. 2 (summer), pp. 23–29.

Moore, B. 1989. *Growing with Gardening.* Chapel Hill, N.C.: University of North Carolina Press.

Moore, R. C., et al. 1992. *Play for All Guidelines: Planning, Design and Management of Outdoor Play Settings for All Children.* Berkeley, Calif.: MIG Communications.

Morris, W. (ed.). 1981. *The American Heritage Dictionary of the English Language.* Boston: Houghton Mifflin.

Morteveille, B. 1942. *The Rose Unpetaled: St. Therese of the Child Jesus* (translated by Mother Paula, O.S.B. St. Cecilia's Abbey, Isle of Wight). Milwaukee, Wis.: Bruce Publishing Company.

National Public Radio University of the Air. 1997. Quotation from Robert Frost, March 2.

Nightingale, F. 1873. *Notes on Nursing: What It Is and What It Is Not.* New York: D. Appleton.

Obernolte, D. 1983. Presentation on the Fibonacci Sequence as It Relates to Landscape Architecture and Nature. University of Minnesota Department of Landscape Architecture, St. Paul, Minn.

O'Neill, M. 1991. A Biologically Based Model of Spatial Cognition and Wayfinding. *Journal of Environmental Psychology,* vol. 11, pp. 299–320.

Ovitt, M. 1996. The Effect of a View of Nature on Performance and Stress Reduction of ICU Nurses. M.A. thesis, University of Illinois at Urbana-Champaign.

Paine, M., and C. Francis. 1990. Hospital Outdoor Spaces—Healing. In C. Cooper Marcus and C. Francis (eds.), *People Places.* New York: Van Nostrand Reinhold, Ch. 7.

Pera, A. 1997. Personal interview concerning integrative healing practices. Mill Valley, Calif., September.

Perrine, L. 1988. *Literature: Structure, Sound and Sense,* 5th ed. San Diego, Calif.: Harcourt, Brace and Jovanovich.

Post, S. 1992. *Behavioral Symptoms in Alzheimer's Disease: A Look Ahead. Alzheimer Disease and Associated Disorders,* vol. 6, no. 2. New York: Raven.

Preiser, W. F. E., J. C. Visher, and E. T. White (eds.). 1990. *Design Intervention: Towards More Humane Architecture.* New York: Van Nostrand Reinhold.

Regnier, V. A. 1985. *Behavioral and Environmental Aspects of Outdoor Space Use in Housing for the Elderly.* University of Southern California, Andrus Gerontology Center.

Regnier, V. A. 1994. *Assisted Living Housing for the Elderly: Design Innovations from the United States and Europe.* New York: Van Nostrand Reinhold.

Relph, D. 1990. People Plant Council Conference. Blacksburg, Va.

Relph D. (ed.). 1992. *The Role of Horticulture in Human Wellbeing and Social Development.* Portland, Oreg.: Timber.

Rico, G. L. 1983. *Writing the Natural Way: Using Right Brain Techniques to Release Your Expressive Powers.* Los Angeles: J. P. Tarcher.

Rothert, G. 1994. *The Enabling Garden.* Dallas, Tex.: Taylor.

Rothert, G. 1995. Make It a Bloom Year. *Mainstream: Magazine of the Able-Disabled* (April), pp. 27–35.

Rothert, E. A., and J. R. Danbert, 1981. *Horticultural Therapy for Nursing Homes, Senior Centers, Retirement Living,* Chicago Horticultural Society, Glencoe, Ill.

Saint-Exupéry. 1943. *The Little Prince* (translated from the French by K. Woods). New York: Harcourt, Brace and World.

Schneekloth, L. H. 1987. Advances in Practice in Environment, Behavior and Design. In E. Zube and G. Moore (eds.), Advances in Environment, Behavior and Design, ch. 12, pp. 307–335.

Sloane, P. D., and L. J. Matthew. 1990. The Therapeutic Environment Screening Scale. *American Journal of Alzheimer's Care and Related Disorders and Research,* November/December.

Sommer, R., and B. B. Sommer. 1986. *A Practical Guide to Behavioral Research.* New York: Oxford University Press.

Stoneham, J. 1990. Sheltered Landscapes. *Landscape Design,* no. 189 (April), pp. 17–20.

Stoneham, J., and P. Thoday. 1996. *Landscape Design for Elderly and Disabled People.* Woodbridge, Suffolk, U.K.: Garden Art Press, a division of Antique Collectors' Club, Ltd.

Susman, G., and R. Evered. 1978. User Participation: An Assessment of the Scientific Merits of Action Research. *Administrative Science Quarterly,* vol. 23, pp. 582–603.

Taylor, T. N. 1927. *Saint Therese of Lisieux, the Little Flower of Jesus.* New York: P. J. Kennedy.

Tuan, Y. F. 1980. Rootedness Versus Sense of Place. *Landscape,* vol. 24, no. 1, pp. 3–8.

Tyson, M. M. 1986. The Essence of Home: Designing Outdoor Environments for Long-Term-Care Facilities. Undergraduate thesis, University of Minnesota at St. Paul.

Tyson, M. M. 1987. Memories of Grandma's Backyard. *Journal of Therapeutic Horticulture,* vol. 2, November, pp. 26–35.

Tyson, M. M. 1989. Pieces to the Puzzle: Environments for Alzheimer's Patients. Unpublished paper, University of Illinois at Urbana.

Tyson, M. M. 1990. Tracing the Wanderer's Path. Unpublished paper, University of Illinois at Urbana.

Tyson, M. M. 1992. The Role of the Outdoor Environment in the Care of Older People with Alzheimer's Disease. M.A. thesis, University of Illinois at Urbana.

Tyson, M. M., and S. Maghakian. 1989. Gardening as Therapy. *Minnesota Horticulturist,* October/November, pp. 24–29.

Tyson, M. M., E. S. Weideman, and J. Anderson. 1990. Unpublished questionnaire survey, University of Illinois at Urbana.

Ulrich, R. S. 1984. View through a Window May Influence Recovery from Surgery. *Science*, vol. 224, April, pp. 420–421.

Ulrich, R. S. 1992. How Design Impacts Wellness. *Healthcare Forum Journal*, September/October, pp. 20–25.

Ulrich, R. S., et al. 1991. Stress Recovery During Exposure to Natural and Urban Environments. *Journal of Environmental Psychology,* vol. 11, pp. 201–230.

U.S. Department of Health and Human Services (DHHS), National Institutes of Health (NIH). 1983. *Medicine for the Layman: Brain in Aging and Dementia.* Bethesda, Md.: NIH publication no. 83-2625.

U.S. Department of Health and Human Services: Public Health Service—National Institutes of Health. 1986. *Hope through Research.* Bethesda, Md.: NIH.

U.S. Department of Health and Human Services, National Institutes of Health. 1992.

University of Surrey, Department of Computing. 1997. Fibonacci Numbers and the Golden Section. http://www.mcs.surrey.ac.uk/personal/R.Knott/Fibonacci/fib.html.

University of Wisconsin, Milwaukee Department of Architecture, 1997. Program description for PhD program in architecture: Environment-behavior studies, Milwaukee, Wis.

Uzzel, D., and K. Lewand. 1990. The Psychology of Landscape. *Landscape Design,* no. 189, April, pp. 34–35.

Van Ravensteyn, F. 1995. Correspondence with curator of St. Dimpna-en Gasthuismuseum concerning history of the treatment of the mentally ill. Gheel, Belgium.

Von Miklos, J., and E. Fiore. 1968. *The History, the Beauty, the Riches of the Gardener's World.* New York: Random House.

Warner, S. B. 1994. *Restorative Gardens: Recovering Some Human Wisdom for Modern Design.* Paper to be reprinted in an upcoming publication by N. Gerlach, R. Kaufman, and S. B. Warner.

Weber, D. O. 1995. Environments That Heal. *Healthcare Forum Journal,* compendium.

Wedge, 1996. *History of St. Dymphna.* Mount Vernon, N.Y.: Franciscan Mission Associates.

Weidemann, S., et al. 1982. Residents' Perceptions of Satisfaction and Safety: A Basis for Change in Multifamily Housing. *Environment and Behavior,* vol. 14, no. 6 (November), pp. 695–724.

Weisman, G. 1983. Environmental Programming and Action Research. *Environment and Behavior,* vol 15., no. 3 (May), pp. 381–408.

Westphal, J. M. 1997. The Role of the Landscape Architect in the Health Care Delivery System. Unpublished research paper, Michigan State University at East Lansing.

White, J. 1997. Golden Ratio. California State University, Monterey Bay, Calif. http://ike.engr.washington.edu/math-wright/book_pgs/book014.html.

Whyte, W. H. 1980. *City and the Social Life of Small Urban Spaces* (film). New York, Municipal Art Society of New York.

Wisner, B., Stea, D., and Kruks, S. 1991. Participatory and Action Research Methods. In *Advances in Environment, Behavior and Design,* vol. 3, Plenum Press, New York, ch. 8.

Zeisel, J. 1984. *Inquiry by Design: Tools for Environment-Behavior Research.* Cambridge University Press, New York.

Zeisel, J. 1997. Buildings in Use. Residential housing model to be reprinted in an upcoming publication. Carlisle, Mass.

Zeisel, J., J. Hyde, and S. Lefkoff. 1994. Best Practices: An Environment-Behavior (E-B) Model for Alzheimer's Special Care Units. *American Journal of Alzheimer's Care and Related Disorders and Research,* vol. 9, no. 2 (March/April), pp. 4–21.

Zeisel, J., and M. M. Tyson. 1997. Unpublished behavioral research study, Hearthstone Alzheimer Care, Lexington, Mass.

Zick, C. 1994. What, Me Worry: Professional Liability for Landscape Architects in the 1990s, pt 2. *Landscape Architecture News Digest,* vol. 36, no. 3, p. 6.

Zimring, C. 1995. *A Guide to Conducting Healthcare Facility Visits.* Martinez, Calif.: The Center for Health Design.

Zube, E., and G. T. Moore (eds.). 1987. *Advances in Environment, Behavior and Design,* vol. 1. New York: Plenum Press.

Zube, E., and Moore, G. T. (eds.). 1991. *Advances in Environment, Behavior, and Design,* vol. 3. New York: Plenum Press. .

Zube, E., and G. T. Moore (eds.). 1991. Wisher et al.'s Participatory and Action Research Methods. *Advances in Environmental Behavior and Design,* vol. 3. New York: Plenum Press.

INDEX

About the Author

Martha Tyson is the principal and owner of Ageless Designs, Inc., Bailey's Harbor, Wisconsin, a firm specializing in the research and design of outdoor spaces for the purpose of restoring the mind, spirit, and body. The architect of many healing outdoor spaces, she holds a B.L.A. in landscape architecture and an M.L.A. with a focus on Environment-Behavior Studies. Martha is also an associate designer with Douglas Hills Associates, Inc., a landscape architecture firm located in Evanston, Illinois.